Florida's Crisis in Public Education

Changing Patterns of Leadership

Arthur O. White

A Florida State University Book

UNIVERSITY PRESSES OF FLORIDA Gainesville

The illustrations in this book are reprinted by permission of the original publisher and the artist:

FEA ACTION, page 62; *Jacksonville Journal*, Oliphant, page 72; *Miami Herald*, page 68; *Miami News*, Don Wright, pages 36, 76, 102; *Orlando Sentinel*, Dunagin, pages 59, 71; *Pensacola News-Journal*, Earle Bowden, page 48; *Pensacola News-Journal*, Brett, page 6; *St. Petersburg Times*, Jim Ivey, page 51; *Tampa Tribune-Times*, George Stewart, pages 56, 66; *Tampa Tribune-Times*, George White, page 3.

The publication of this work was supported by a grant to Florida State University by the State of Florida Department of Education, Contract Number 750-083.

Library of Congress Cataloging in Publication Data

White, Arthur O.   1942-
    Florida's crisis in public education.

"A Florida State University book."
Includes bibliographical references and index.
    1. Public schools—Florida—History. 2. Decision-making in school management. I. Title.
LA258.W48   379.759   75-11968
ISBN 0-8130-0516-7

Contents

Preface

Patterns of state educational leadership in Florida have been altered in recent years through economic, social, and political upheavals. Between 1948 and 1957 Florida reached a high point of cooperative governance of education. In those years the chief state school officer and the head of the Florida Education Association often cooperated in developing and lobbying for legislative educational programs.

During the 1959 legislative session, however, disruptive forces first appeared that were to plunge the school system into a crisis of factionalism culminating in the nation's first statewide teacher strike in 1968. The aftermath of the crisis was chaos. And student radicalism and federally mandated school desegregation in the early 1970s led the legislature and the governor, together with the chief state school officer, to come forward during the next five years to repattern the educational leadership of Florida. Their overhaul of the school system included an ambitious program of comprehensive planning and funding equalization that was able to pull the system back together.

The underlying cause of the 1968 crisis was inadequate funding. Educators were humiliated by their low salaries, hindered by shortages of supplies, and even endangered by decrepit and overcrowded schools. They demanded explanation of and improvements in their situation. Through the actions of county and state teachers associations they labeled as their tormentors selfish politicians in a legislature unfairly apportioned to favor rural North Florida counties. These leigslators protected an industry-biased, regressive, and inelastic state tax system and an indefensibly low county valuation schedule, which together guaranteed the inadequacy of funds for education.

Impatient for relief, a faction of militant teachers demanded immediate reform. State leaders would have preferred to go about improving matters slowly and diplomatically. Unrelenting, the militant leaders among the teachers adopted increasingly provocative measures. These actions achieved some success on the county level and brought most of the state's teachers to the militants' side.

Immediately the legislature and the governor lined up in opposition to the educators—even while partisan politics left them at odds with one another. In this degenerative atmosphere militant teachers, losing all hope for an acceptable legislative compromise, went out on strike. During the strike, the chief state school officer held to a moderate course, trying to bring the dissident elements together for a settlement favorable to the schools.

Eventually the strike proved disastrous for the teachers. Forced back to work without gaining significant concessions and penalized by county school boards, they lost their power base. A leadership void was filled by a repatterend partnership of cooperative governance. A reapportioned legislature met frequently on educational issues, and a governor friendly to education enabled the chief state school officer to administer progressive education programs.

This study of changing patterns of leadership and

decision making in education was supported by the State of Florida Department of Education. The Department of Education has taken the position, wisely in my judgment, that understanding of past triumphs and failures in the administration of public education can improve the quality of present-day decision making. Knowledge of recent history may thus contribute to our understanding of where we are and how we got there; such knowledge can also suggest what should be done or avoided to get us where we want to go.

Any historical study is dependent for its quality on the richness of available source materials. This study has benefited from the collection of thousands of documents concerning education in Florida made by Howard Jay Friedman. As a public relations expert during the terms of several chief state school officers, Friedman organized a treasure trove of materials relating to education in Florida. Countless details of this history were recovered from the materials in his collection and from interviews on his experiences as a participant in many of the events highlighted in the study.

Above all I would like to thank my wife Tana Lee for her devoted commitment to my work. Throughout the entire period of this study she stayed close to my side as research assistant, typist, editor, critic and morale booster. Thanks, too, are extended to the many people who sat patiently and graciously for lengthy interviews on their dynamic roles in Florida education.

Chapter One
Roots of Crisis

B Y OCTOBER 1965, when Thomas D. Bailey retired after seventeen years as state superintendent of public instruction, the influential coalition of elected state officials, legislators, civic leaders, and professional educators that he had helped to forge in order to place Florida schools among the leading school systems of the nation had split apart. Born in a tiny South Carolina hamlet in 1897, Bailey at age twenty-four took a teaching position at a DeFuniak Springs Methodist preparatory school. In 1948 with experience as a teacher, principal, supervising principal, and president of the Florida Education Association (FEA), he was drafted by a committee of prominent Floridians to run for state superintendent of public instruction when the incumbent Colin English decided to make the race for governor.[1]

During his second year in office, Bailey began to publicize Florida's "education crisis." In a radio address recorded for distribution across the state as well as in speeches to service clubs, the superintendent listed the state's most critical problems as inadequate financing, a shortage of classrooms, a shortage of elementary school teachers, and inferior schools for blacks.[2]

The only elected official charged with the guardianship of the entire state's educational interests, Bailey moved to resolve the crisis. His opportunities for leadership were several: he took part in major policy decisions, reached by a majority vote in the State Board of Education (composed of the governor and four elected Cabinet members) of which he was the secretary; he served as a member of the state Cabinet, which reviewed all types of important state business; he developed school legislation and took primary responsibility for a staff of education specialists who dealt with problems affecting the entire school system as well as some difficulties limited to a single district or a single school. Confronted by a host of pressure groups both in and out of government, the state superintendent acted as a stabilizing force to keep the schools operating at near their maximum potential.[3]

Bailey's principal associate in formulating changes in the system was his close friend Ed B. Henderson. Appointed executive secretary of the FEA upon Bailey's decision to run for the state superintendency, Henderson headed an organization with 80 to 90 percent of the state's teachers and administrators as members. He also served as an officer for the state School Board Association, composed of all county school board members, and as advisor to such education minded civic groups as the Continuing Education Council, the Council of 100, and the Florida PTA.[4]

Bailey concentrated on steering a good school program through the legislature, while Henderson worked persistently on behalf of teachers. The superintendent and his staff developed a legislative program for each biennial session and reviewed it with key legislators and before legislative committees. Henderson usually led a team of popular teachers to argue for education bills. Unlike Bailey, Henderson seldom made speeches but tactfully encouraged the FEA's annually elected president to act as spokesman. Together with their organizations, these two leaders collaborated on most school legislation to form what became known as the Florida school lobby.[5]

Initially they sought to strengthen Florida's Minimum Foundation Program (MFP). Enacted in 1947, the MFP served as a model for similar programs in forty-four other states. In Florida, the MFP distributed most state school funds according to each county's taxpaying

The legislature examining the schools on how they had measured up to the expectations of the Minimum Foundation Law during its initial two years of application.

ability, the number of instructional units, and the type of instructional activity; typically fund allocations were based on a goal of one teacher for every twenty-seven students in average daily attendance. Each county school board was encouraged to enrich its school program beyond the minimum funded by state allocations by levying up to ten mills in property tax and by calling on the freeholders periodically to vote up to ten additional mills. To ensure that the 1949 Legislature adequately funded the program, Bailey and Henderson disseminated information on its advantages and held frequent discussions with the lawmakers during the session. The resulting $89,000,000 appropriation, $52,000,000 more than appropriated by the previous legislature, jumped per-pupil expenditure from $170 to $294, provided large salary increments for teachers, and guaranteed a 180-day school year; it also confirmed that Bailey and Henderson were a potent combination in the public education programs of the state.[6]

The influence of the school lobby reached its zenith in 1957 when the legislature voted record increases for education. After a statewide campaign to show the critical needs of education caused by the state's spectacular population growth, the State of Florida Department of Education (DOE) and the FEA, with important help from legislators, developed an educational program appropriation package stipulating large increases in capital outlay for classrooms and hefty salary increases for teachers. The legislature responded favorably to a recommendation from Florida's Community College Council for six new junior colleges. The Community College Council had been charged by the previous legislature with developing a master plan to put a junior college within commuting distance of every Floridian. Bailey, who had instigated the establishment of the council, endorsed community colleges because they would both raise the educational level of the community and overcome the obstacles of distance and scarce resources that prevented most rural young people from attending college.[7]

The leadership provided by Governor LeRoy Collins added to the momentum. First elected in 1954 to fill the unexpired term of a deceased incumbent, Collins with strong support from the school lobby became Florida's first governor to succeed himself and did so by winning the nomination in a first primary. Collins, who believed that an outstanding educational system invigorated by a junior college program offering technical training would attract industry to the state, advocated in his opening message to the 1957 Legislature higher taxes to fund six new junior colleges, increased classroom construction, and higher teacher salaries.[8]

The legislature responded with hearty endorsement, designating that the first $36,000,000 collected from Florida's 3 percent sales tax be used for education. This revenue together with that from other tax sources yielded a $115,000,000 annual increase for an educational plan that increased the state's proportionate contribution to Florida's total school fund to an all-time high of 57.7 percent, over 20 percent more than what it had been a decade earlier. No wonder Bailey praised the plan as a "Magna Carta for teachers and children in Florida."[9]

Of this money, $23,000,000 went directly for classroom construction; $36,000,000 went to relieve rural classroom shortages by matching an equal amount raised locally. Funds also became available for driver education, for education of exceptional children, for vocational education, and for adult education. With the establishment of six institutions under a separate junior college MFP, Bailey was honored as the father of Florida's junior college program. With teachers gaining a

salary increase of between $300 and $1500 yearly, the
FEA was declared Florida's most influential educational
group, and its executive secretary was ranked among the
hundred most influential Floridians. Nationally, the
state's reputation had soared. The *New York Times*

Don't Close Our Schools!

A reminder to legislators that only those ignoring their con-
sciences would use the segregation issue for political gain by
supporting last resort bills to close public schools of districts
required by the federal government to desegregate their schools.

education editor cited Florida for "the greatest improvement in the nation at every level from grammar schools through the graduate courses at state universities."[10]

Almost immediately, however, economic recession and school desegregation reversed these encouraging trends. By the time the legislators had returned for the 1959 session, Florida's boom had slackened during an economic recession that affected the entire nation. A shock wave of economic disasters had slowed the state's burgeoning population growth, curbed the building industry, reduced tourism, increased drastically the number of foreclosures—all such events serving to wipe out fortunes made only a few years previously during the prosperity of the mid-1950s. Understandably, the legislators expressed a mood of "no new taxes," "hold the line on spending," and, even worse, "retrenchment."[11]

If the austerity program was to succeed, it became particularly important to limit spending on education severely. In Florida, schools had been absorbing around sixty cents of every general revenue dollar. Floridians, however, had paid the price willingly because the school lobby had built up a strong commitment to education.[12]

This commitment might have carried the school system safely through the economic storm if controversy over impending school desegregation had not been building in the legislature. Since soon after the Supreme Court had declared school segregation unconstitutional, Bailey, Collins, and Henderson with help from Attorney General Richard Ervin and many legislators followed a moderate policy of lawful avoidance. Foreseeing eventual desegregation, these men considered legal means to delay the action, as Bailey put it, "to prepare for gradual effective adjustment to desegregated schools." In 1956, after Collins had won the primary nomination for governor over three "rabid" segregationist candidates, the moderates passed a pupil assignment law.

Designed to delay desegregation without bringing federal retaliation, this law avoided any mention of race to stipulate that pupils be transferred between schools only if they matched the moral, psychological, and socioeconomic background of the pupils in the school of admission. Such provisions would, it was expected, bar most black children from white schools.[13]

Unappeased was a block of ultra segregationists mostly from twenty-two rural North Florida counties. By reason of the most unrepresentative legislative apportionment system in the nation, legislators from sparsely settled areas composed a majority of both houses. Protecting this system was a clique of rural county senators, dubbed the "Pork Chop Gang" after voting for "pork" (selfish interests) when negating Collins's attempts in 1955 to make the legislature more representative of the population.[14] With mostly small farmers as constituents, who overwhelmingly endorsed ultra segregationist candidates, rural county representatives made every effort to retain the dual school system.[15] Before they could act in 1956 on an interposition resolution for using state power to nullify the federal desegregation decision, Collins became the first governor in Florida's history to resort to constitutional maneuvering to terminate a legislative session.[16]

Prospects for a strict segregation bill improved greatly by the opening of the 1957 session. Enjoying the advantages of a statewide uproar over the expected qualification of a few blacks to attend white schools under the pupil assignment law and the power of their partisans occupying the presidency of the Senate and the speakership of the House, the ultra segregationists won early passage of an interposition resolution. Collins again intervened to label the act "a hoax" after sending it to Congress with a denunciatory message. But the ultra segregationists retaliated with "a last-resort bill" enabling a vote of 25 percent of the property holders in a district threatened with desegregation to abolish the public schools. Believing that the schools must be preserved even if it meant integration, Bailey made an impassioned plea to prevent this "blow against the bedrock of democracy." Collins followed with a blistering veto of what he called "not the last-resort bill, but the first resort of the agitators."[17]

This veto seemed final until President Dwight Eisenhower commanded federal troops to desegregate Little Rock Central High School and the Supreme Court struck down Virginia's pupil assignment law. During a special session in October 1957 ultra segregationists planned to repass the last-resort bill. After returning from a conference with Eisenhower on mitigating southern tensions, Collins, bolstered by Bailey and a more moderate House Speaker, aligned thirty-one legislators to defeat the last-resort bill again.[18]

Unfortunately, the continued success of the school lobby on the segregation issue helped foment a legislative bolt from the education coalition during the 1959 session. Arriving for the session, the ultra segregationists prepared to avenge the action of the moderates. Aware of their sentiment, Collins opened the legislative session with a strong statement against the school abolishment bill: "never, never, never set up any plan or device by which our public schools can be closed." Heartened by such leadership, the school lobby not only prevented thirty-seven drastic segregation bills from becoming law, but stymied moves for a special session to revise the Constitution to include a school closing provision.[19]

Although the staunchest segregationists admitted defeat, their well-publicized campaign induced Floridians to see the schools as potential bastions of dangerous racial liberalism. This development, along with increasing economic pressure, contributed to a skepticism about the value of supporting public education. Responding to the people's mood for austerity, interim legislative committees preparatory to the 1959 session made the most searching investigation of Florida's system of public education in history. After hearing from one of these committees, the lawmakers, labeling many education programs initiated by the 1957 Legislature "frills," reduced MFP funds by five million dollars below estimated needs, the first reduction since the MFP had been enacted. Teacher salaries remained at 1957 levels, and the school lobby received negative responses to many of its requests.[20]

Only the new junior college program escaped the parsimoniousness of the session. Because the state would provide the majority of the funds, and because the technical education phase of junior college programs promised to train an abundance of skilled workers, almost every legislator eagerly sought a junior college for his county. The legislators' enthusiasm was intensified by the national recognition that the proliferation of junior colleges was bringing to Florida and by the positive response of industry outside Florida to the colleges' technical and vocational programs. The legislature authorized $7,437,360 for increasing the number of junior colleges so that by September 1960 a college education would be within commuting distance of 58 percent of the population.[21]

While this program sold itself, Bailey and Henderson concentrated on the less popular and more expensive segments of public education. Meeting with legislators almost daily, school lobbyists began issuing frequent bulletins on their progress. Although lawmakers contemplated more cutbacks, a "united front of the educators" convinced them to yield $33,400,000 in additional funds to continue at current quality the education program for the first grade through high school (1−12) despite increased enrollments. Included in this money was fourteen million dollars obtained by reducing the number of exemptions from the sales tax.[22]

Some observers, however, considered Bailey's defeat of the "red textbook bill" his most outstanding accomplishment. This measure sought to bar from the classroom, regardless of the topic or sentiment of the authors, all books and materials written by Communists and persons on subversive lists. Those opposed to censorship were gratified when Bailey testified before a House committee that he deplored the bill's reflection on the patriotism, loyalty, judgment, and honest motives of not just the twelve thousand teachers involved in Florida's textbook rating system but on all Florida teachers to be restricted by the bill in their choice of supplemental classroom materials. The superintendent also saw the bill as an "attempt to close the minds of children to our everyday problems." The committee agreed and thwarted the so-called "book burners" in their attempt to interfere with the public schools.[23]

Feelings of distrust nevertheless began to develop between educators and legislators. Resentful of Bailey and Collins for undermining the segregation campaign, ten rural county senators, the most prominent of whom was former governor Charley E. Johns, drew a resolution condemning Bailey and Collins for undue interference with legislative process. Picking up on this sentiment, the press noted that the school lobby had used the vote recruiting potential of the state's thirty thousand teachers and their allies to wield "an iron fist over one-third of the House of Representatives." When talking to professional education societies, Bailey admitted to anxiety during "the roughest legislative session" he had ever experienced: "We must know and vote our convictions for the good of the children. If we are not the most powerful lobby in the State, then God help us."²⁴

In 1961 when Farris Bryant took over the governorship, conditions for the schools deteriorated even further. In striking contrast to his predecessor LeRoy Collins, who had made excellent schools the capstone of his campaign for economic growth, Bryant believed that a restrictive tax base would much better achieve this result even if it meant a mediocre school system. This position could be attributed to the influence of Bryant's most powerful backers, leading Florida industrialists. With North Florida legislators also depending on the support of these industrialists, the governor and the legislature, if not always agreeing on just where to make budget cuts, usually exhibited general agreement that spending must be kept as low as politically feasible.²⁵

Accompanied by their wives and seated at desks adorned with flowers, legislators listened while Bryant advocated what one reporter called "down to the bone economy" to save the state fifty million dollars. He told the assembly that his record-breaking $771,982,424 budget would allow a $184,016 surplus because of the state's economic growth. Insisting that "money alone will not educate," Bryant warned that the state could not afford to spend seventy-five million dollars for a $750 across-the-board teacher raise advocated by both Bailey and Henderson. Instead, Bryant wanted a far less costly merit raise system that together with plans developed by his committee on quality education would ensure "maximum utilization of personnel, facilities, pupils, and time to achieve the highest quality in public school education."²⁶

Although obtaining support from several legislators for more school tax money, Bailey and Henderson generally met stiff opposition. Reminding the governor of his call for economy, legislators cut two million dollars from Bryant's textbook request, severely limiting the state's free textbook program. In turn, the governor vetoed $9,500,000 for capital outlay funds, deleting $7,900,000 for existing junior colleges and $282,104 for a new junior college in Orange County. Also school libraries and educational television were removed from Bailey's program. Despite Henderson's best efforts, teachers would receive a guaranteed raise of only two hundred dollars with an additional four million dollars being distributed from an optional merit raise fund affecting about one-fifth of the faculty. As part of this latter proposal, all counties were required to keep careful records of teacher effectiveness. Moreover, any teacher seeking tenure or promotion would need a score of 500 on the National Teacher Examination (NTE) and any veteran teacher seeking to qualify for a five thousand dollar minimum yearly salary would need ten years of continuing service, ruling out teachers who lost time because of illness or pregnancy.[27]

Still, as in the previous session, the school lobby had some effect. Spurning sentiment for retrenchment, the legislature fully funded the grades 1 through 12 under the MFP, continued to match local funds for classroom construction, and allocated money to open at Boca Raton Florida's first upper-division university. Toward the end of the session, Bailey dissuaded the conference committee from adding to the appropriations bill a rider providing that any federal money in aid of teachers' salaries would displace, not supplement, an equal amount of state money. Although diplomatically praising the legislators for awareness of school needs, Bailey pointed out that because of the no-new-tax pledge all attempts to obtain higher taxes for the increasing needs of education had failed.[28]

Educators also continued to deal with extremist

groups that were undermining public confidence in the schools. A legislative investigating committee, known as the Johns Committee after its chairman Charley E. Johns, refused to believe that professional educators could be depended upon to police their own ranks. Designated by the 1957 Legislature to look into Communist infiltration of the schools, this committee, without apparent authority, had begun gathering information on homosexual teachers. Appalled at some of the committee's methods, Bailey defended the rights of the accused teachers and publicly refuted charges that the schools were refuges for practicing homosexuals.[29] While contending with this problem, Bailey successfully modified an Americanism versus Communism bill from a right-wing measure requiring high school seniors to learn the advantages of capitalism over "Communistic enslavement" to a law requiring a course on the comparative dynamics of both systems. Refusing to be compromised, members of patriotic societies leveled charges that Communist influences had infiltrated state textbooks. As before, the superintendent defended Florida's system of choosing textbooks so ably that he thwarted efforts at censorship.[30]

The state having recovered economically, the school lobby made modest headway with the 1963 Legislature. Preparations had begun early with frequent reports to Bryant's Quality Education Committee and to interim legislative committees on education. On March 18, 1963, Bailey distributed his report on financing the MFP. Having detected a trend of decreasing proportional state support for the MFP, Bailey warned of deteriorations in school programs of thirty-five counties already levying millage to the legal limit. In 1961 the situation had become so critical that the legislature had placed a 5 percent ceiling on the amount of increased county financial obligation for the MFP. Yet the state's MFP funding share had fallen 3 percent to 72 percent of the total, 10 percent below the state's best record set in 1957. Fearing more deterioration in the next two years, Bailey noted that to maintain existing levels of education quality under the then current state-local division of funding responsibility would require an impossible 30 percent increase in county funding compared to only a 5 percent increase for the state. Bailey asked that the legislature stop withdrawing at the state level school funds put in at the county level by setting a 75-to-25 state-to-county funding ratio for the MFP with the state allocating a larger share if a county's share increased by more than 5 percent.[31]

Bailey also concentrated on obtaining a better textbook appropriation. Using the same approach, the state superintendent found that since 1955 a $10,500,000 shortage had developed in the state textbook program, resulting in thousands of children sharing worn and outdated textbooks. He backed up his assertions with data from a Department of Education survey team reporting on thirty-eight counties with severe textbook shortages.[32]

Apparently impressed by these arguments, Governor Bryant opened his final legislature with recommendations for a teacher salary raise, a ten million dollar appropriation for textbooks, a sixty-seven million dollar addition to the MFP, and a fifty-eight million dollar addition to capital outlay funds for junior colleges. To pay for it all, he wanted an extension of the 3 percent sales tax to virtually every commodity except groceries and medicine. Although Bryant's endorsement of merit raises and of NTE scores upset many teachers, the school lobby influenced an end to the merit system and gained a one-year extension for new teachers to obtain a

National Teacher Examination score of 500. Overall the legislature authorized salary raises for teachers of between $350 and $550, costing the state over forty-five million dollars for the biennium; removed the word "continuous" from the law guaranteeing ten-year veteran teachers a minimum salary of five thousand dollars; set a 75-to-25 state-to-county ratio for the MFP; added $4,364,000 to the textbook appropriation; and more than doubled the previous biennium's appropriation for junior colleges from about nineteen million to forty-three million dollars.[33]

Once more Florida was recognized nationally for advancement in education. In 1963, Bailey received a Freedom's Foundation Award for his pioneering work on the Americanism versus Communism course and Good Housekeeping Magazine cited Florida as one of three areas of the country where concern about outdated books had led to larger textbook appropriations. Bailey's efforts against textbook censorship and obsolete books resulted in the nation's first statewide adoption of the most scientifically sound series of elementary school science textbooks available. When the state superintendent announced that these books had been accepted by the Textbook Committee, sophisticated theories of human evolution and explanations of human reproduction became available not only to Florida's school children, but to children living in many other states soon to follow Florida's example.[34]

These successes, however, proved a flimsy cover for a severely underfinanced school system. Bailey, addressing nine thousand delegates at the FEA convention, emphasized that even the most innovative planning could not achieve quality education without the 1965 Legislature dispensing much more "money" for the schools. In fact, if Florida's school population grew by the expected 5 percent, every dollar would be absorbed from the

$79,500,000 in additional state funds expected to be the maximum granted by the next legislature. Bailey then lectured his audience that Floridians could easily afford to do much more since on the average only 4.1 percent of their personal income went for schools compared to a national average of 4.3 percent. Optimistic as always, Bailey looked for strong leadership from the governor's office to bring Florida back to the forefront nationally.[35]

Disappointingly, Haydon Burns, another governor backed by Florida industrialists, pledged himself to a policy of no new taxes. When opening the 1965 Legislature he proudly related, "I present you a balanced budget." According to him the state was financially so healthy that without new taxes the sales tax alone would raise $110,000,000 more for the general revenue fund, giving the state during the next biennium a $25,000,000 surplus. Noting that at the polls Floridians had endorsed a university construction program and that they strongly supported junior colleges, Burns asked that $176,000,000 be dedicated to university and junior college construction. He alarmed the educators, however, by ignoring the critical financial needs of the rest of public education.[36]

The school lobby attempted to soften the implication of Burns's position. During a meeting with the legislature's Appropriations Committee, the superintendent made a plea that $5,900,000 taken from the MFP be restored, while Henderson argued vehemently for a 1 percent increase in the sales tax to accumulate one hundred million dollars during the next biennium for a $550 to $1100 raise in teachers' annual wages. Turned down by the committee, Henderson told members of the Capitol press corps that if the state wanted to end the teacher shortage and to prevent teachers from moonlighting to feed their families, higher salaries must be granted them. "Everywhere we go," Henderson disclosed, "people say if they could be assured that the money would go toward the education of their children they would pay higher taxes." Subsequently, Bailey and Henderson won headlines with shocking figures that Florida ranked nationally eighth for hospital care, tenth for police protection, twenty-third for fire protection, thirtieth for road expenditures, but thirty-fifth for education.[37]

Burns's successful resistance to this pressure hastened the end of the school lobby. On-the-scene observers described the governor stopping new tax proposals almost effortlessly while inducing legislative endorsement for an industry-biased three hundred million dollar road construction bond proposal to be submitted to the people. Tending the pork barrel, Burns and the antitax faction had killed a sales tax increase proposal by fusing traditional North Florida opposition to high taxes with a growing resentment among South Floridians that the MFP acted as a subsidy to the rural counties that continued to underassess their property and to turn down school bond issues. A more extensive inventory tax, advocated by South Florida legislators as a substitute for increased sales taxes met with the admonishment that such a tax violated Florida's constitutional provision against a state income tax. Consequently, on May 12, 1965, when on an invitation from Henderson some three to five hundred civic, PTA, and school leaders from several parts of Florida gathered to show support for a teacher salary increase bill, House Education Committee Chairman Robert Mann of Tampa stated emphatically: "You know the answer is no. The bill is dead. It's just a question of which committee is going to kill it. You are in the wrong place and on the wrong floor."[38]

Because the school leaders interpreted that statement

to mean that they should go back to the counties for additional funds, Henderson hoped to inspire a grass-roots drive for obtaining salary increases; but the legislature again blocked his way. On May 21, 1965, in a Duval County taxpayer's suit, the state's highest court interpreted Florida's "just value statute" at nearly 100 percent of the estimated market (true) value of property for assessment purposes. Considering the governor's reproval that "a few counties with a ruthless approach to tax assessment can cost the state new industry," the legislature enacted a millage rollback law as a safeguard against sudden tax increases. Henderson, sensing the unfairness of the measure, tried to soothe disappointed teachers with reports that thirty-five counties still planned teacher salary increases, but his young aggressive board of directors on May 22, 1965, called in the National Education Association (NEA) for an investigation of Florida's political atmosphere as a hindrance to public school progress.[39]

This action brought into the open a militant teacher movement that had been rapidly expanding within the FEA. Chafing under instructional salaries that ranked the state twenty-ninth in the nation and under classroom conditions characterized by overcrowding, obsolete equipment, shortages of supplies, and too many extra duties, a considerable number of teachers mainly from the urbanized counties of Duval, Dade, Broward, and Volusia on the east coast and Hillsborough, Pinellas, and Polk on the west coast began to turn the FEA away from Henderson's diplomatic course toward greater militancy. Such teachers had developed strong County Teacher Associations (CTAs) that flourished in communities populated largely by immigrants from northern cities where teachers had active unions and higher salaries. Having secured salaries comparable to the national average from their own school boards, these teachers prepared to confront the legislature and accomplish much more, especially a minimum salary of five thousand dollars a year for all Florida teachers. It was for the good of the children, their spokesman claimed, that teachers organize throughout the state because in fifteen predominantly rural counties, including Leon County, the site of the state capitol, school boards had so intimidated their instructional employees that their CTAs dared not protest salaries often close to the state's lawful yearly minimum of four thousand dollars.[40]

To some observers the new teacher attitude reflected the politics of the '60s, which had already encouraged thousands of blacks, university students, and members of other minorities to take to the streets for redress of their grievances. Others placed the responsibility on thousands of male instructors who had come to Florida from northern school systems. (Florida's teacher training institutions could provide only one thousand of the six thousand teachers needed annually to replenish a teaching corps that grew from nearly thirty thousand to fifty-five thousand teachers between 1959 and 1965.) Still others blamed the FEA parent organization, the National Education Association, which pressured by the American Federation of Teachers sought a dramatic victory to retain the confidence of its members.[41]

The teachers, however, attributed the crisis to the rural dominated legislature that shackled the state with the narrowest tax base of any state in the Union. Contemptuously referring to legislators opposed to their demands as "Pork Choppers," teachers recounted how the rural block had retained its majority through two reapportionment sessions called voluntarily by the governor and two reapportionment sessions required by federal action. This left the legislature in 1965 composed of a Senate to which 14 percent of the state's voters could elect a majority and a House to which 29 percent of the state's voters could do likewise. Understandably, teachers believed that such a legislature would never enact a state income tax or a corporate profits tax, both of which would reach rural Florida's citrus and phosphate industries that were then paying little in taxes. Actually, there was hardly any state tax in Florida other than a 3 percent sales tax with so many exemptions as to leave the wealthiest industries practically untaxed.[42]

In 1965 the state-financed Florida Development Commission attracted industry by advertising that commercial interests paid just 7.8 percent of the total state taxes compared to 15.69 percent in other Southern states and 18.17 percent in the nation. What the commission did not cite was a fact often repeated by teachers that Florida industries had grown so rich in their semitropical tax shelter that they spent an astronomical $350,000 in 1965 for lobbyists during the sixty-day legislative session.[43]

Although they had driven the proportion of state support in Florida's education dollar below 40 percent for the first time in twenty years, the lawmakers during the 1965 session would do nothing to relieve school board dependence on a local tax system riddled with inequities. Protected by a five thousand dollar homestead exemption and assessment procedures as low as 30 percent of valuation in some rural districts, thousands of propertied Floridians paid no school taxes. Moving against this favoritism teachers and other taxpayers supported lawsuits in several counties, but the process of revaluation was too slow, costly, and tedious to overcome the growing impatience of teachers.[44]

Consequently, as Florida grew in prosperity and population, the inequities of the tax system yielded proportionally less and less for schools. Between 1956 and 1966, when the number of public school students shot up from 823,759 to 1,300,000, taking the state from the nation's seventeenth largest school system to its ninth largest, in per capita expenditures on education the state dropped from twelfth to thirty-fourth. Once reputed to be "the best of the worst," for attaining the highest school allocations among Deep South states, Florida fell to fourth from the bottom between 1951 and 1964. This decline had occurred in spite of the state ranking tenth nationally in per capita income in 1964 after accruing over thirteen years a 202 percent increase in total personal income, more than twice the national rate of growth of 92 percent.[45]

The impact of these changes on Florida's teaching profession was devastating. Surveyed in 1964, former Florida teachers representing twenty-five different disciplines indicated that by leaving to teach in other states or by leaving the profession entirely each one of them had gained at least $350 in salary with most receiving $2,000 or more. Significantly, the largest jump of $4,600 to a figure doubling the Florida salary was made by an elementary teacher who transferred to the Michigan school system. Moreover, less than half the two thousand teachers yearly graduating from Florida universities accepted teaching positions in the state, and results from a questionnaire returned by four hundred education majors at state schools indicated that in 1964 54 percent of them had no intention of teaching in Florida unless the base salaries increased substantially. One result was that principals, unable to fill 789 teaching positions by the time of the pre-school planning conferences in August 1964, suspended personal interviews during a frantic recruiting drive that put 389 untrained teachers in the schools and still fell short by 350 appointments.[46]

Whatever the causes of teacher militancy, the approaching NEA investigation heightened tension dramatically. With two weeks to go in the session, lawmakers denounced the FEA for trying to blackmail or blackjack them into voting teacher pay raises and authorized a special teacher recruiting drive to offset any unfavorable publicity generated by militant teachers. At a University of Florida workshop over one thousand PTA members listened in subdued silence as Robert Mann provoked FEA President-elect Robert Jones of Ocala with condemnation of the FEA for using unprofessional methods to serve teacher interests rather than quality education. Jones retorted that it was the politicians who were robbing the state of quality education with their no-new-tax stand and who had forced the FEA to call for an investigation. Once aware of the problem, Jones asserted, Florida citizens would demand solutions from the legislature, removing the necessity of national sanctions against the state. Disagreeing, the Florida School Board Association expressed bitter disappointment that outsiders had been invited to Florida when the state should be allowed to solve its own difficulties.[47]

All the while teachers, engaging in provocative actions, tarnished their public image as professionals wanting only "to share their abilities for the benefit of mankind." Full-page advertisements in county newspapers illustrated teacher grievances, and Leon County teachers planned to organize their own investigation. Whenever a hundred or so teachers got together, they displayed their enthusiasm with standing ovations punctuated with whistles, cheers, and a rebel yell or two. CTA officers in Dade, Hillsborough, Volusia, Marion, and Polk counties, occasionally referring to their CTAs as unions, inspired their followers to impose "nonteaching sanctions" until school boards granted higher salaries and better working conditions. More than a threat, nonteaching sanctions meant for teachers the censure of school board members, withdrawal of summer school services, and boycott of extracurricular activities. Impressed that the seven thousand member Dade County

Teachers Association had invoked such tactics to coerce their board into salary negotiations leading to a thousand dollar annual raise, FEA members brushed aside admonishments from Bailey and Henderson that such brash moves divided school officials, teacher groups, and parents "into three armed camps all fighting and squabbling among themselves." With little hope of rebuilding Florida's school coalition and given an outstanding business opportunity, Bailey gave up his office in October 1965, ending the longest tenure of continuous service for any state superintendent in Florida's history.[48]

Chapter Two
Gaining a Truce

D ESPITE A deepening crisis, Floyd Christian, the man appointed by Burns to complete Bailey's unexpired term, vowed to make Florida schools "second to none in the nation." Born on December 18, 1914, at Bessemer, Alabama, Christian moved with his family to a Pinellas County dairy farm during the height of the depression. Having distinguished himself as a University of Florida football player and as a teacher and coach at a Pinellas County high school, a decorated World War II veteran, Christian in 1948 was drafted to run for the office of county school superintendent. Victorious in a tough three-man race, Christian for the next sixteen years led Pinellas County schools to national recognition. Never losing a millage election nor having the voters turn down a bond proposal, he had raised thirty million dollars to finance forty new schools for a student population that had grown from twenty to eighty thousand. In 1952 when the Republicans were swept into most Pinellas County offices, Christian was the lone Democrat to retain his position, eventually winning endorsement for reelection in 1956 from the Republican school board and becoming in 1960 Florida's first appointed county school superintendent. In 1959 he gave the state a hint of his style when newspapers headlined "Christian Explodes on Legislature." From the platform of the state PTA meeting in Gainesville, Christian had laid it on the line, describing the 1959 Legislature "as one of the worst" for depreciating the excellent educational advances started by the previous session.[1]

Christian took state office as an advocate for the children of Florida ready to bring the resources of the Department of Education to bear even in local disputes. Among his first actions was to involve himself in Duval County's supercharged fight over school appropriations. On October 30 all extracurricular activities ceased when the Duval County Teachers Association called a work slowdown to protest a $7,800,000 holdback of school funds recommended by the Duval County Budget Commission. His statements, rife with "political risk," convinced the board to retain all but $1,600,000 of the original budget, an action that provided adequate funds to ensure Duval County teachers an average raise of eight hundred dollars and adequate standards for reaccreditation of county high schools.[2]

Praised by the press, radio, and television, the new superintendent confidently began a campaign for better school funding. Sometimes speaking twice a day before service clubs, PTAs, professional organizations, education groups, and at dedications of academic buildings, he hoped to reverse the discouraging trend of taxpayer protest against 100 percent assessments. He had detected this trend when a hundred thousand persons voted zero mills for schools and when residents of ten counties voted millage below school board requests.

Wavering local support meant for Christian a new era in which the state had to assume the major share of education funding. To meet the challenge he recommended a 1 percent increase in the sales tax to assure funding for a five thousand dollar minimum yearly teacher salary. Still he thought the citizens should know that more sales taxes for schools did not mean the end of ad valorem property taxes: "Good schools cost money, but poor schools cost more. There is no such thing as a cut-rate education."[3]

The superintendent's zeal favorably impressed Governor Haydon Burns. At Christian's urging, plans moved ahead for a two-day Governor's Conference on Quality Education, which attracted two thousand persons to Tampa on February 24, 1966. Dubbed the "Burns-Christian thrust for better schools," Christian opened the meeting with his speech "Reaching for Greatness." Although confident that the state's fifty-six thousand teachers, despite the crushing school population of 1,287,000 pupils, could make the state an educational leader, he cautioned that morale was rapidly deteriorating under instructional salaries that averaged $228 below the national average for elementary and secondary school teachers, $1,200 below the average for junior college teachers, and $717 below the average for university teachers. Christian climaxed his presentation with twenty-four statements supporting his belief that education must be the first responsibility of state government. He advocated that the state henceforth provide: the major share of school funding; minimum teacher salaries of between five and eight thousand dollars a year; standards insuring accreditation for every elementary school; kindergartens in every county; and "above all the best education that money can buy."[4]

The hundreds of congratulatory telegrams, requests from service clubs for as many as a hundred copies of the address, and widespread favorable press comment showed that Christian had hit a responsive chord among his fellow citizens. His popularity had reached such proportions that several challengers for his elective office withdrew from the contest. The most serious of these aspirants, Fred Karl of Daytona Beach, known as "Mr. Education" during three previous legislatures for his handling of both the FEA and Department of Education legislative programs, endorsed Christian for a courageous stand on educational finance. The only Cabinet officer unopposed for election in 1966, Christian was proving the truth of his slogan, "the best politics is a good education program."[5]

Most important was the attitude taken by the FEA. While commending Christian for dynamic leadership, FEA news dispatches criticized Burns for his conference theme "A Revolution in Florida Education by 1976," which ran contrary to teacher demands for action now. Burns drew further skepticism by promising to finance a minimum teacher salary of five thousand dollars without new taxes and by appearing to use his Conference on Quality Education for political purposes.[6]

On March 10, 1966, the NEA investigating team reported on the "political atmosphere in Florida." A group of fifty educators, laymen, and members of the news media heard Florida teachers characterized as "underpaid and intimidated" into working in schools riddled with inadequacies. These conditions had been fostered by a rural dominated legislature that held 19th-century notions of economy and aggravated by the governor's insistence that the state stay within current tax levies. Investigators also found teachers frustrated by officials raising objections about tapping for education sources of money potentially available at every level of government. These officials put off the teachers with such arguments as: taxes on real estate are already too high; increased state support means new taxes and there must be none; and federal support brings federal control and we must shun this evil. Concluding their report, investigators suggested that the state stop procrastinating and develop a Quality Education Program

(QEP) to replace the MFP with "realistic quality levels of support."[7]

Following the presentation, a question and answer session turned into an hour and a half of angry debate. The NEA team coordinator likened the report to a "baton we have given the people of Florida to make use of for its own worth." FEA President Bob Jones for one did not think it was worth much because it failed to set blame for Florida's education ills directly on the 1965 administration and legislature. In answering Jones, the president of the state PTA received scattered applause for her assertion that the governor and members of the Cabinet were elected by "we the people on a no-new-tax slate. . . . if we want more money for education, we are going to have to pay taxes for it." As the hour ran past 10 p.m., FEA members withdrew for private study of the report.[8]

Out in the state aroused teachers echoed dissatisfaction with the report. During crowded meetings they wanted to know why the investigators had only offered an insipid mass of statistics as opposed to a report demanding sanctions, blacklists, and other means for exerting pressure on politicians. Substantially in agreement with the teachers, FEA Board members, after weeks of deliberation, placed Florida on "sanction alert," warning that if conditions reported by the NEA continued beyond the 1967 legislative session, the FEA would invoke state sanctions and request national sanctions. These actions would make it unethical for teachers to move between counties for employment purposes or for any teacher residing outside the state to migrate to Florida for employment.[9]

That teachers should engage the state in open battle forced a difficult dilemma on Christian. A strong ally of teachers, Christian who in 1955 had been one of the few administrators ever elected president of the FEA on the sponsorship of his CTA, wanted neither to undermine the teachers nor to divide the state further. Instead, while giving notice that he sought to rectify many of the objectionable conditions enumerated in the NEA report, the superintendent asked teachers not to alienate public support so crucial to any increased benefits for education.[10]

After Burns's defeat in the May 1966 primary, Christian looked for leadership from Florida's next governor —either Democrat Robert King High, mayor of Miami, or Republican Claude Kirk, Jacksonville investment banker. Kirk acted first, promising Christian in June 1966 "to work for our prime goal of the number one education system in the nation." Christian advised both candidates that "to get the support of educators you must come up with a realistic way to finance educational improvements with state funds."[11]

Kirk used his talks with Christian and other Cabinet officers as a basis for a series of "White Papers" detailing his plans for running state government. Endorsing many of Christian's recommendations, Kirk shaped a fifty-two page report around the theme "Florida First in Education." In reviewing how studies had been made, one on top of the other, showing that county taxes on real estate had reached the limit, Kirk promised "action now and not more studies." Within the first year of his administration, he promised that the state role in funding education would be increased to make possible minimum teacher salaries of between five and eight thousand dollars; reading disability programs; county kindergarten programs; vocational education within reach of every child; computer assisted instruction and construction of innovatively designed classrooms. However, Kirk troubled Christian and the teachers with pledges to achieve educational advancement with no new taxes. His strategy was to stretch the tax dollar by reducing "wasteful bureaucracy" in public education and distributing state funds gleaned from the state's economic growth only to counties engaging in innovative planning rather than pumping more money into an already poorly administered school system.[12]

Although the election of Kirk gave Florida another governor pledged to austerity, the Department of Education and the Florida Education Association saw promise in the 1967 Legislature being the most representative in Florida's history. Following a federal court order to reapportion both houses before July 1, 1965, as required by the Supreme Court's decree of one man, one vote, the 1965 Legislature after its regular session had returned for twenty-five days of haggling that led to reapportionment breaking the "stranglehold" of rural Pork Chop Club members. During another extraordinary session called by Burns under federal pressure in March 1966, urban county legislators (lamb choppers) had further increased their representation; but the Supreme Court in January 1967 overturned this plan for another designed by a political scientist that gave fourteen urban counties a clear-cut majority in both houses of the state legislature.[13]

To encourage public optimism, Christian stressed the positive aspects of the situation. He proclaimed 1967 the big year of decision when the legislature might enact a billion dollar school budget financed by a 1 percent increase in the sales tax. Asked how he planned to deal with Kirk's no-new-tax pledge, Christian played down the governor's assertion by referring to other Kirk promises "to get the money."[14]

The educators also tried to maintain a hopeful outlook. Stronger than ever by reason of a merger with the all-black Florida Teachers Association, the FEA now having fifty-one thousand members, among them sixty-five hundred administrators, was a "third political force." While aspirants to the legislature campaigned for votes, FEA leaders counseled their members to make sure candidates stood right on education before making a choice at the polls. The teachers also prevailed upon Henderson, who had wanted to retire with Bailey, to try once more for a legislative solution.[15]

These improving prospects for a compromise seemed only to evoke bellicose acts from the state's flamboyant governor. The first Republican elected governor in ninety-four years, Kirk had capitalized on new political conditions. Since World War I immigration had decreased the proportion of registrered Democrats to registered Republicans in the state, while dividing the Democrats between the liberals, mostly from urbanized South Florida, and the conservatives, mostly from rural North Florida. To hold out against the Republican challenge, conservative Democrats in 1961 had changed the date of the gubernatorial election to divorce it from national civil rights politics, making Haydon Burns a two-year governor. This stratagem failed when in 1966 Burns lost in the primary to the liberal Robert King High, prompting the conservatives and business interests to unite in electing Claude Kirk governor of Florida.[16]

Instead of dividing the Democrats further, Kirk inadvertently pulled them together by his "politics of confrontation," a style characterized by "standing up to your opponent." Not only did Kirk, like some other Florida governors before him, resent the scheme by which the governor shared administrative responsibilities with six Cabinet members, but he faced the added difficulty that these men were Democrats. At his inauguration, Kirk shocked many Democrats by announcing plans to call the legislature into special session for preparing a new constitution to accomplish, among other things, a Cabinet appointed by the governor. Kirk, a vice-presidential hopeful, looked forward to making more headlines by tangling with organized teachers whose coercive tactics daily added to their unpopularity.[17]

At a series of governor's conferences, Kirk named himself "commander-in-chief" in a war on ignorance that would make Florida education number one in the free world, but then brashly reasserted his no-new-tax stand and promised to hold the minimum teacher salary below five thousand dollars until 1969. Interpreting these tactics as "playing politics with the education of our children," Christian told a hundred teachers at Kirk's final conference on April 25, 1967, that the governor had gone back on his White Paper promise of setting base salaries between five and eight thousand dollars. Chirstian concluded that anything less than total cooperation from the governor was to invite a teacher shortage so bad it would create chaos and turmoil.[18]

Instead of responding to this urgency, Kirk brought the state closer to sanctions by more callous treatment of the assembled teachers. After emphasizing in his "tell-all" address that he wanted the "thinking of teachers," Kirk promptly cancelled a discussion session and withdrew from the hall. In the afternoon, he showed up at small-group teacher sessions, but avoided answering any questions, saying that they should be submitted in writing for the evening session. Anxious to hear Kirk's answers, the teachers waited patiently for hours, but the governor never appeared or sent word. Totally frustrated, the teachers returned to their CTAs to report on "this dismal final fizzle."[19]

Kirk had pushed the compromise hopes of Christian and Henderson into the path of a grinding FEA militancy. While the governor held conferences, FEA militants put together a $495,000,000 legislative program to include $275,000,000 for teacher raises, $25,800,000 for junior college faculty raises, $59,800,000 to reduce teacher-pupil ratios and $51,000,000 to give teachers thirty minutes for lunch and thirty minutes for planning as well as a professional negotiations statute allowing collective bargaining, an improved teacher tenure law, and an elimination of millage elections. Backing up their demands with sanction workshops, they discovered the magnetic power of appeals for unity in the face of Kirk's showmanship. In March at the FEA convention thousands of teachers, hearing Kirk portrayed as the arch enemy, responded to an appeal from the FEA president that they stand and link hands as a symbol of solidarity.[20]

The teachers were therefore ready when on April 17, 1967, the governor in his budget message to the legislature warned that he would not impose any additional tax burdens, essentially cutting the heart out of the FEA legislative program requiring a substantial increase in state and local taxes. The legislature reacted by passing two appropriation bills, one reflecting the governor's pledge to spread a teacher raise over two years and another reflecting a Department of Education plan to raise the sales tax by 1 percent for financing an immediate teacher raise. Although Christian and Henderson by lobbying aggressively had obtained enough bipartisan pledges to override a veto of the Department of Education bill, FEA directors, before the governor had acted on either bill, invoked sanctions on May 24 in the form of "(1) public censure of Governor Claude R. Kirk, (2) national circulation of notice that Florida is an unsatisfactory place to teach, and (3) request that the NEA take supportive action."[21]

This was indeed a brash gesture as reapportionment had kindled an unprecedented surge of Republican legislative strength to back the governor. In two years the percentages of Republicans in the Senate had gone from 5 to 42 percent and in the House from 9 to 33 percent. Plunged into partisan politics by the FEA's most challenging action yet taken against their party leader Governor Kirk, Republican legislators accordingly sustained the governor's vetoes of $132,000,000 in education appropriations leaving the teachers with the governor's salary plan and the state with three dollars less to spend per pupil than during the previous biennium.[22]

Kirk's vetoes touched every part of education. So many dollars were stripped from the junior college program that only an extended session of the legislature prevented financial ruin of the colleges. In fact, neither campaign promises nor advice from the governor's own conference on education could stop Kirk from scuttling plans for new universities at Miami and Jacksonville and from rejecting a one million dollar industrial services training program.[23]

Sanctions signaled the ascendency of Phil Constans as executive secretary of the Florida Education Association. With a Ph.D. from the University of Florida the thirty-nine year old Constans, as a student, teacher, and administrator had experienced Florida education from the early grades through high school and the university. Forced like many teachers to work sometimes under miserable conditions, he had responded with good spirit and good humor, but he began to resent strongly the familiar adage "those who can't do, teach." In light of such public attitudes, Constans felt, teachers could only gain concessions by banding together to use drastic means, even a strike. Henderson, who stayed on until July 1967 to assist the new executive secretary, recalled Constans's satisfaction that he now headed a powerful organization capable of closing the schools. Christian also knew Constans, having nominated him for president of the FEA in 1956 and having stood with him on the same platform to denounce the legislature in 1959.

'AN APPLE FOR TEACHER'

A well-fed Governor Claude Kirk presents to the hungry teachers of Florida only the core of a state school budget. The Governor had recently injured his arm in a baseball game put on as a publicity stunt.

Then a lobbyist for the FEA, Constans had related how he hated his serf-to-master relationship with legislators. He longed for the bitter satisfaction of meeting a legislator in public debate because "as equals, when you took a swing at me then I would verbally kick your teeth in." Constans believed that "the fight is between the teachers and the so-called power structure of the state. You just have to look at who's driving the train to see who's killing education."[24]

As expected under Constans, sanctions, mass meetings, and the threat of mass resignations typified the FEA's relationship with the state. Immediately after the sanction order the new executive secretary rallied two thousand teachers for a legislative information day to denounce Kirk's teacher salary plan as a "sop" since it would take two years to attain a five thousand dollar minimum salary and would be gained only by taking money from such excellent programs as school lunches, textbooks, and kindergartens. At sanction rallies across the state, teachers viewed a seventeen-minute color film of Constans beseeching them to close their eyes and link hands, "You're at the moment of truth, you're not alone, the teaching profession will never be the same again." In the background the orchestra played "Impossible Dream."[25]

On June 4 the FEA announced a hundred thousand dollar national campaign to discourage the movement of business, industry, and teachers to Florida. A day later, the NEA, with over one million members, declared national sanctions against the state. This action inspired the FEA to oppose practically every Floridian; Kirk was denounced for "blatant irrationality," Republican legislators were described as "puppets," the public was "indifferent." and Floyd Christian was a "sell out."[26]

Floridians responded in kind. The governor labeled the FEA the anti-Florida Education Association headed by Constans, who "brainwashed teachers into attacking our state, our children, and our parents." The legislature also reacted strongly, taking the Professional Rights and Responsibilities Commission away from FEA control in order that it not be used to coerce teachers into honoring sanctions. Thousands of letters to the governor generally expressed the indignation of hard-working Floridians at the FEA's business sanctions undermining the economy and at teacher demands for beginning salaries set higher than amounts often earned by men with families after sometimes twenty years of employment.[27]

FEA leaders met the situation with an all-out "persuasion drive" for a special session of the legislature exclusively devoted to substantial improvements in public school financing. To spearhead the drive, Constans unveiled the FEA's plans for mass resignations. FEA leaders had devised this stratagem because of teacher reluctance to adopt such labor tactics as a strike. They needed a more professional alternative, and mass resignations seemed to be the answer. Moreover, this scheme might hold up in court against Florida's statute forbidding strikes by public employees. School boards too would be restrained by mass resignations because teachers could easily leave Florida considering that the NEA listed 170,000 unfilled instructional positions nationally. As the *St. Petersburg Times* put it, "if schools close, recruiters from other states will pounce on Florida's good teachers with offers to fill vacancies in their states."[28]

Proclaiming a professional information day, the FEA scheduled a mass rally at the Orlando Tangerine Bowl on August 24, 1967, to launch a drive for undated teacher resignations. Constans, who was unsure of the turnout, remembers a heady feeling when he looked out and saw an estimated thirty thousand supporters awaiting him.[29] They clapped, whistled, and cheered sometimes with tears streaming down their faces as he exhorted them, "we will not practice our profession where teachers are not respected and children are not important." As their leaders spoke FEA workers moved up and down the aisles collecting resignations and distributing bundles of provocative literature.[30]

The momentum of the teacher movement reached a peak. Thousands of teachers streamed out of the Tangerine Bowl for more boisterous rallies in their home districts. The FEA with a bursting treasury distributed thousands of "confidential memos" on resignation procedures and financed trips for its lieutenants to lead the rank and file at their rallies. By September 21 the FEA was predicting that thirty thousand teachers would turn in resignations in a drive costing between two and three hundred thousand dollars, of which ninety thousand came from a voluntary sanction fund and another fifty thousand from the NEA.[31]

Teachers reached out for community support. Wherever they went teachers spoke about Florida's deepening crisis, even accompanying their bill payments with leaflets accusing Floridians of utter irresponsibility for inadequately funding public education. Moreover, by extensive neighborhood canvasses, protesting teachers came face to face with Floridians.[32]

Apparently the persuasion drive began to have the desired effects on public opinion. Although the FEA planned to keep secret the exact number of resignations, press leaks indicated high percentages of resignations in most urban counties contributing to resident appeals to the governor for a special legislative session. Constans, at last getting a chance to debate a legislator, exchanged angry words with a leading Republican senator before hundreds of Jaycees at their annual convention. Feeling that he had been received cooly, Constans welcomed news that this ordinarily conservative organization had refused to pass a resolution condemning the FEA for invoking sanctions.[33]

On September 4, 1967, two thousand teachers in Pinellas County struck the first blow by turning in their resignations directly to the school board. Resigning teachers demanded that the school board yield higher pay and a resolution on behalf of a special education session of the legislature.[34]

Scoffing at the teacher activities as "voodoo meetings for the purpose of hand-holding and chanting," Kirk pronounced that there was no crisis in education and therefore no urgency in calling a special session of the legislature. On September 5 the governor on statewide television walked down the corridor of a Tallahassee elementary school, entered a classroom to write on the board "Perspectives for Tomorrow," his plea for patience while he made Florida schools foremost in the nation. To prove his no-crisis theory, Kirk cited figures that the state spent sixty-seven cents of every general revenue dollar on education, that the 1967 Legislature had authorized the largest teacher pay raise in the state's history, and that Florida ranked ninth nationally in total expenditures on education. He then stated that "money alone would not solve Florida's education problems," which had been brought on by "educrats" building Chinese walls around education to hide inefficiency. From allegedly thorough investigations he had found this inefficiency in "the state's lack of a master plan to achieve long-range education goals: in teacher salary raises granted without stipulations that teachers be accountable for their work, and in an outdated DOE guided by an elected superintendent reduced by partisanship to an elected politician, who together with an impotent State Board of Education had fostered the development of sixty-seven separate county educational empires."[3][5]

The situation could only be reversed, concluded the governor, if the people trusted him to face down blackboard power advocates in the teacher union which had subjugated the schools. To facilitate his campaign Kirk asked that the people grant him the right of appointing a citizen superboard of education which as part of its duties of supervising all of public education would choose a state school superintendent. This plan would make possible such innovations as complete state financing of education, state sponsored consolidation of the sixty-seven county school systems into much larger units, state development of a smaller but more efficient DOE to monitor county school systems with "grade measurement," "computer technology," and "cost control." He announced formation of a thirty-citizen Quality Education Commission to develop a master plan for making Florida first in education by 1975. Until his Quality Education Commission completed its fifteen-month study, Kirk saw no justification for a special session.[3][6]

Hardly had Kirk's image faded from the television screen when twenty-eight hundred teachers in Broward County followed the lead of their colleagues in Pinellas County by resigning en masse for higher pay and a special session of the legislature on education. Unable to operate the schools with only seven hundred of its four thousand teachers reporting to work, the Broward County School Board on September 7 declared a three-week school shutdown. After this period the system faced loss of state funds affecting ninety thousand children, 7 percent of Florida's school population. A week later, however, the school board obtained a court order forcing teachers back to work, but not before Broward's all-Republican board had agreed to endorse a special session, set up a grievance committee, and grant a $158 across-the-board raise.[37]

The results in Pinellas County also enhanced the teachers' power. With resignations from nearly all county teachers stacked on his desk and his school board seeking a court injunction, the county school superintendent's negotiations for a settlement went nowhere. Instead the teachers, forced back to work by a court order after one day out, wore black arm bands and staged a work slowdown. They won such concessions from the Republican dominated school board as its endorsement for a special legislative session and salary increases averaging $579 per teacher, pushing the county average above the national mean by $460 and making the county's salary schedule the second highest in Florida.[38]

What Broward and Pinellas county teachers associations had accomplished in Constans's estimation was a vanguard for any statewide action. Their victories had proven the ineffectiveness of legal action against resigning teachers and served as a warning that the absence of professional negotiations nurtured the conditions for a walkout. Turning to a possible strike, Constans cited a startling number of resignations held by his office and indications that the persuasion drive was increasing popular support for FEA demands that the legislature convene for an education-finance session by the first of November; that the Senate President and House Speaker name a bipartisan committee to consult with teachers on education needs as a basis for a finance program to be enacted by the special session.[39]

Through it all, Kirk stuck to his political course. Maintaining that there was little to be concerned about, he announced plans to honeymoon in Europe for two weeks with his German-born bride, but Broward's school board chairman began burning up the lines to the governor's office pleading for advice on how to get off the FEA hot seat. Advised by his aides to keep out of Broward County, Kirk drafted a news release attacking Broward's twenty-eight hundred resigning teachers for being duped by national agitators and denouncing Christian for collaborating with the "teacher union." Before it was released, he toned down his message concerning Christian to a characterization of the state superintendent as a "do-nothing" at a time when Florida should take the lead in stopping a national pattern of teacher rebellion. Once in Europe, he telephoned his top aides in Broward County daily to prevent a school board capitulation, even if it meant employing all substitute teachers. By an open letter in the newspapers he provoked Christian's resentment with embarrassing reminders that the state superintendent must do his duty of requiring teachers to honor their contracts and of keeping the schools open.[40]

Kirk's entire plan backfired when the state press castigated him for foisting yet another study on the beleaguered school system before abandoning the state for a frivolous pleasure trip.[41] Upon his return, he admitted to there being a serious situation, if not a crisis. Hastily conferring with school board members from Broward and Pinellas counties, he promised a series of sixty-seven separate school board conferences for devising sixty-seven separate yardsticks to be used by the Quality Education Commission in developing a single standard of evaluation for the entire school system. Continuing his emphasis on local solutions, Kirk dramatically reversed his stand on property tax relief to promise a campaign in the counties for increased school millage. He also promised to raise new state taxes if voted for by the people in a referendum.[42]

Few trusted the governor's new course of action. State reporters saw his discussions with Republican school board members as an attempt to solidify Republican opposition to a special session. Regarding a tax referendum, Kirk was generally interpreted as wanting the people's mandate either to back down on his no-new-tax stand or to renew it with their support. Teachers, however, saw only the danger that public opinion might be used by the governor to defeat additional school taxes.[43]

As the governor began to feel pressure from his opponents, high-level Republicans came to his defense. In their estimation, Kirk struggled against a national conspiracy by the Democratic oriented NEA to embarrass Republican governors. It was no accident, they said, that the FEA had chosen heavily Republican Broward and Pinellas counties as test areas for their bellicose methods. As evidence they cited frequent FEA phone calls to NEA headquarters during Broward County's strike and the eruption of similar actions by NEA affiliates in Utah, Oklahoma, New York, and Michigan —all, like Florida, under Republican governors.[44]

Democratic leaders mounted a scathing counterattack. For these men any conspiracy could be traced to Kirk's causing a "gullibility gap" by twisting figures and describing teachers as an "intellectual mafia." Democratic chiefs felt that Kirk was a governor in name only, that he was manipulated by William Safire's New York public relations firm, which had been hired at ninety thousand dollars a year by the Florida Development Commission to merchandise Kirk to the American people "like toothpaste."[45]

Christian maneuvered between the various factions. Receiving reports from his two top staff members on the scene in Broward County that Kirk's people had sought to block their efforts at compromise, Christian wondered if the governor wanted a mass teacher walkout so that he could enhance his national image by breaking it. On a Tampa television station, Christian lambasted Kirk for bringing Florida to the brink of disaster with unnecessary delays in coping with the school crisis. By the same reasoning, Christian saw Kirk's personal attacks on him and his office as part of a scheme to get rid of at least one Democrat Cabinet member.[46]

The superintendent felt differently about Florida's protesting teachers. When Constans described them as "fed up" with delapidated schools, crowded classes, crowded busses, insufficient materials, outdated textbooks, inadequate equipment, and inadequate pay, Christian agreed with him. When Constans described them as not primarily interested in salaries, but instead dedicated to "children through action," he also agreed with him. However, when Constans cited thousands of resignations as evidence that the teachers would close the schools if the needs of education were not "met and met now," Christian disagreed with him. He believed that most teachers would have second thoughts about breaking their contracts, disrupting their lives, and abandoning their pupils.[47]

Few people shared Christian's viewpoint. Estimating that as many as fifty thousand teachers might respond to an FEA strike order, the press warned that if the special session was not forthcoming teachers might "virtually shut down the public school system." To lend emphasis to their warnings these reports cited the Broward and Pinellas county confrontations as well as the important role played by Florida educators in the national trend toward teacher strikes. For example, Janet Dean, president of the Dade County Teachers Association, received wide publicity in July for leading a drive that persuaded the NEA to reverse its no-strike provisions with pledges of funds, legal advice, and staff assistance to striking affiliates. According to Dean such an action was "typical of the NEA change from the reluctant dragon to a dragon that's in charge."[48]

Short of advocating a walkout, Christian gave strong support to the FEA persuasion drive. He joined with Constans to advocate a state income tax although he knew "there was a lot of political death in it." Describing FEA sanctions as justifiable in light of the governor's vetoes, he had asked that teachers be given leave to attend the FEA Orlando rally; and citing the black arm bands of Pinellas County teachers, he pleaded for a solution short of court order because "you can't force a teacher to teach."[49]

He risked political repercussions on September 19, 1967, to put up $1,672 of his own money to share air time with Constans on fourteen television and five radio stations for a rebuttal of Kirk's "Perspectives for Tomorrow" speech. Constans led off with a polished video taped performance of himself walking down the same Tallahassee elementary school corridor that Kirk had used in his presentation, but writing on the blackboard "Perspectives for Today." As he talked a film of the Orlando rally appeared before the cameras; Constans explained that these were teachers who had come through the night by car and by plane to show resolve that there "is a crisis in education." Then to discredit the governor's assertions that the state was ninth in expenditure, Constans cited other figures that the state stood thirty-fourth in per-pupil expenditure and spent only twenty-nine cents of its total revenue dollar on education.[50] When discussing teacher grievances, he said little about salaries but stressed the teachers' desires for more involvement in decision-making, more planning time, and more qualified colleagues to reduce the classroom load.[51]

With only fifteen minutes to make his points, Christian appearing in person hit from the shoulder. He deplored the governor's duplicity in subtly attacking local control and initiative by promoting state financing and budgeting for county school systems after having just vetoed $132,000,000 of critical state aid for education. Such action as the governor had taken, the superintendent noted, further reduced the state's proportionate contribution to Florida schools. During the past decade, Christian estimated, the state had cut its share of Florida's education dollar from 59 to 41 percent resulting in double sessions for thirteen thousand students, in a shortage of fifty-two hundred classrooms, and in classes for eighty-five thousand students being scheduled in halls, corridors, libraries, and lunchrooms, and "worst of all—the possibility of resignations by the majority of our sixty thousand teachers." "The solution," he told his audience, was for "the legislators and governor to come back to Tallahassee and complete the job of financing education."[52]

Nevertheless, as memories of FEA triumphs like the Orlando rally faded and the governor's efforts to minimize the importance of the situation took effect, public opinion began to waver. Trying to reverse these trends, the FEA with aid from the superintendent publicized that the schools would be open on Sunday, October 1, so Floridians could see for themselves the depressing conditions. Reacting quickly, Kirk implored school boards to refuse teachers access to the schools while demanding a county-by-county account of the costs of such an operation. With half the counties following the governor's lead in refusing to open the schools, teachers ready with petitions for a special legislative session waited, mostly in vain, for parents on school steps, athletic fields, and in parking lots. Judging Crisis Sunday a "flop," Constans threatened to activate the resignations to break public apathy, but restrained by his board instead announced another Orlando rally for FEA members to vote on a course of action.[53]

Convinced that open communications would bring

about a constructive resolution sooner than threats and counterthreats, Christian sought a means to end the dangerous impasse between the governor, the FEA, and the legislature. At his urging a bipartisan legislative committee composed of ten Democrats and four Republicans including two strong Kirk supporters and at least two FEA advocates began meeting to discuss the education crisis. According to committee chairman House Speaker Designate Fred Schultz of Jacksonville, the committee would be an action committee to concentrate on reconciling the Republican minority to a special legislative session on education.

The success of this venture, however, depended on softening the hard line taken by the governor. At a series of conferences, Kirk had refused to relinquish his eighteen-month timetable for a special session while Constans just as stubbornly demanded a special session in December to take precedence over the governor's pet projects of constitutional revision and tax reform. Impatient of the stalemate, FEA President Dexter Hagman, who had attended some of these discussions, told newsmen on October 6 that the FEA would activate teacher resignations if an accord was not reached prior to a mass teacher rally scheduled for the Tangerine Bowl on October 22.[54]

Hagman had taken a decisive step. In effect, what he had done was to assert that an estimated thirty-two thousand teachers, by turning in undated resignations, had signed over their professional lives to the few men who ran their professional organization. Teachers had been led to believe that they would return to Orlando on October 22—labeled "D Day" for day of decision—to vote on whether to activate their resignations.[55]

A spoof on the Florida Education Association's Crisis Sunday indicating that every day was a crisis for Florida education, about to be exploded by volatile politics.

Indeed, some FEA directors had misgivings about a walkout. Foremost in their minds was uncertainty as to how many of those submitting resignations would actually walk out, leaving the possibility of the number of participants falling below 50 percent of the teaching force, the percentage thought crucial to paralyze the schools. There was also a problem of poor participation in the rural counties, where school boards were in a position to accept resignations promptly from those few teachers ready to walk out though aware their docile colleagues would keep the schools open anyhow. Aside from these considerations, concern had been growing about a hostile public reaction. Already warned by the Crisis Sunday setback, FEA leaders had reports that public resentment against the detrimental effects of business sanctions had grown so strong that the voters would reject requests for increased school millage. As one reporter put it, "anytime an organization tries to keep business, industry, and conventions out of the state it is going to incur a lot of animosity." Hagman had nevertheless preempted all options, and the FEA as well as the county teachers associations sent out procedures for a walkout.[56]

With the state bracing for a strike, Christian tried to calm county school officials by counseling them on how to react to the crisis. As representative of the people, Christian asked that school officials make every effort to keep the schools open. He further cautioned officials not to accept mass resignations but to follow the law in requiring each teacher to submit a separate resignation and to inform those teachers that unless the school board accepted their resignations they faced a one-year suspension of their license for leaving their classrooms. Still, Christian repeated his position that "the only way to solve the situation is to have a special session and do an adequate job for education."[57]

Receiving Christian's directives, county school boards made preparations for using substitute teachers to take over classrooms in the event of a strike. Sometimes pressured by county boards, principals began sending letters asking for parent volunteers. Supplementing this

Kirk crossing his fingers while shaking hands with the Florida Education Association hoping that their agreement would end the struggle over school financing.

action with radio and newspaper advertisements, school officials expected to be able to replace about 10 percent of the teaching force.[58]

Anxious to end the rush toward a walkout, Christian two days after Hagman's ultimatum set up a meeting between Constans, Schultz, and several members of the bipartisan committee, among them the Republican Senate leader. Although extreme tension was evident, the legislators acknowledged that they believed Constans to be a moderate, not a "real bad guy," a militant leader. Tipped off either at this meeting or at a subsequent meeting with the bipratisan committee that Kirk would only be reasonable if dealt with privately and alone, Constans on October 16 began marathon negotiations· with the governor. Around midnight Kirk told Constans "you've got to lift statewide sanctions, end the threat of mass resignations, and call off the mass teacher meeting." Constans agreed on condition that Kirk call a special session, which the governor conceded for January 1968.[59]

Constans relayed the information to Schultz. Describing a teacher strike as potentially the most critical and frightening crisis of his lifetime, Schultz intensified negotiations until receiving tacit approval for the compromise from all members of his committee at 2 a.m. on October 17. Later that morning at a press conference, Hagman formally called off the Orlando rally. A smiling Governor Kirk followed with the rest of the agreement so as to appear not to have acceded to a threat. Shaking hands with Hagman, Kirk congratulated himself, the superintendent, and the FEA as the three elements most concerned with education.[60]

The reaction in the state was "thank God, no walkout." By noon of October 19 news of the settlement moved from school to school. The chairman of the Palm Beach County School Board found it good to hear "that the forces of reason and conciliation have unlocked the school crisis." Interrupting his address, the windup speaker for a convention of secondary principals received applause for his conclusion "that the teacher unrest which prompted the controversy was a step toward and not away from professionalism." Citizens quoted by the media strongly expressed their relief and happiness over the settlement.[61]

Chapter Three

A Short Truce

ENTERING A period known as the "truce," Floridians looked to Kirk's Quality Education Commission for a resolution of the crisis. With only eighty days until the special session, instead of eighteen months as previously expected, the commission chairman declared a crash schedule and replaced with state personnel the New York firm originally contracted to consult on the master plan. Including persons from the universities, the Department of Education, the governor's staff, the FEA, the Board of Regents, state agencies, private business, and private foundations, these educational experts were acutely aware of a need for decisive action since recently voters in nineteen counties had returned zero mills for schools meaning cutbacks in county programs if the state did not come through with more money.[1]

The thirty business and professional leaders of the commission worked through six committees, each with a staff support team: business and industry; elementary and secondary education; higher education; finance; legislation; and public information. The support team totaled fifty educators who in turn employed another thirty of their colleagues as consultants. Acting as coordinator for the 130 persons who packed themselves into the commission's cramped "nerve center" of legislative offices was an executive committee embracing such disparate elements as Constans, Deputy Superintendent of Education John Seay, and the governor's Chief Education Advisor Charles Perry.[2]

The support team of educators known as the "brain trust" proved difficult to control. Skeptical of Kirk's insistence that there was no problem with the schools so pressing that long-range goals should not be emphasized, the educators warned that they would not participate in a whitewash. They felt that if the committee overlooked the immediate issues of more tax monies for the schools and professional negotiation procedures for teachers it would be "standing in potential rubble contemplating utopia."[3]

In the midst of controversy the commission proceeded with public hearings. At Miami, the commission heard the executive secretary of the Dade County Teachers Association assert that to make available enough tax money for schools the commission must find a way to end prohibitions against a state income tax and a corporate profits tax. Dade's school superintendent pointed out that Florida property taxes were not nearly as high as those of several other states and that tax yields in his county, for example, would not overcome a fourteen million dollar loss in local revenue precipitated by the last legislature's restrictions on the inventory tax. Meeting at other troubled spots, the commission often stayed late into the night to hear suggestions, complaints, and proposals from educators and laymen.[4]

The commission also dealt with important data from Schultz's bipartisan committee. Reporting in November 1967 Schultz's group compared Florida with ten states of similar size as well as with other southeastern states. In the national sample, six states built more new classrooms than Florida in 1965–1966 and only three states had more children on double sessions. As if it were not critical enough that Florida's tax revenues per one thousand dollars of personal income fell below the

Kirk was depicted so indifferent to the work of his own Governor's Commission on Quality Education that its final report had to be parachuted to him while he vacationed at a Colorado ski resort.

national average and below that of three states in the comparative sample, the state also had the lowest percentage rise in teacher salaries during the previous decade among all states of comparable size.

Florida's poor national record could be traced to the inability of county school boards to withstand the squeeze of rising costs, rising enrollments, and rising teacher strife on the one side and falling state support on the other. Their resources spread too thin by these pressures, school boards in twenty-four counties reported making severe reductions and in another twenty-four counties making mild reductions in their programs to give teachers even a small annual raise. These cutbacks produced overcrowded classrooms in twenty-seven counties, overcrowded busses in forty-seven counties, book-sharing for pupils in thirty-four counties, and no kindergarten program in forty-eight counties. The entire report pointed to a chronic need for substantial increases in state support of education.[5]

The master plan finally presented by the commission to the governor on December 22, 1967, combined important new suggestions with many ideas long advocated by educators. Essentially it called for reorganization of the educational structure on all levels; simplification and improvement of education finance; more state support coinciding with required limits on local support from ad valorem taxes; locally developed plans for educational improvement subject to state approval; local programs for staff development; elimination of district millage elections; comprehensive school construction programs; introduction of modern management techniques; twelve-month utilization of staff and facilities; expansion of the junior college and university programs; and development of a plan to provide education tailored to Floridians from preschool age through senior citizens.[6]

While finding much merit in the report, Christian took strong exception to a provision that an appointive state superintendent be the first priority in restructuring the school system. Christian noted his experience as both an elected and an appointed school superintendent to illustrate that the state position should remain elective. According to him an elected superintendent possessed the prestige of Cabinet membership which together with an election mandate from the people enabled the superintendent to pursue an independent course. Recognizing Kirk's political motivation, he especially abhorred the idea of appointment by the governor.[7]

When Kirk in his opening message to the special session on January 19 threatened to wield the veto pen if the legislature did not restructure the system under a governor appointed superintendent and set a referendum on any new taxes, Christian placed his job on the line by offering to have the people decide on an appointed or elected superintendent. Entering the House chamber at 11 a.m. January 31, Christian became Florida's first Cabinet officer to address a joint session of the legislature. He insisted that unless the legislature "is free to conduct its deliberations unrestricted by threat of veto" he feared "for the future of the free public schools in Florida." Although certain that an unfavorable vote by the people could end his incumbency, he accepted the governor's challenge and urged that an amendment on the question be placed on the ballot.[8]

At all hazards Christian sought to avert a veto of a money bill that might give justice to the teachers. With the press rallying to his side after his speech to the joint session, the superintendent talked educational finance with most senators and representatives. He, believing that a forthcoming referendum on the question of an appointive superintendent amendment would encourage the governor's signature on a large appropriation bill, asked his fellow Democrats to concede passage of the referendum legislation. His staff, working many times until 4 or 5 a.m., helped pro-education senators win a 38 to 10 vote in the Senate for an education package increasing state funds for schools by $267,000,000, which was sufficient for the FEA "to avert mass resignations."[9]

"CLICK!"

This cartoon sought to banish any doubt that the Florida Education Association had coerced the legislature into a special session for January 1968.

The Senate package also represented Kirk's interests. To gain his signature and fulfill the requests of Christian, the senators wrote into the package an amendment for submission to the people removing the state school superintendent and the state Cabinet Board of Education from the constitution. The senators attached to this provision another stipulating that if the amendment succeeded a nonpartisan school board of fifteen citizens appointed by the governor would recommend to the legislature an appropriate structure for supervision of public education. It was generally thought that this scheme might "start Kirk and succeeding governors on the way to almost total control of Florida education."[10]

Despite Christian's describing the bill as the finest legislation ever to come out of a Florida legislature and the FEA warning that a walkout would ensue if the legislation was "diluted too greatly through House-Senate compromise," opposition built up in the House. With constituents angered over sharply rising county property assessments, a block of representatives rallied behind the big-county strength of Duval and Hillsborough demanded millage limits set at twelve mills in exchange for supporting a 1 percent increase in the sales tax, the first addition since the tax was applied in 1949.[11] This demand was immediately interpreted by representatives of Dade, Pinellas, Palm Beach, and Broward counties as risky because of the state's uneven record in supporting education.[12] Strong though they had been in their objections opponents of millage limits agreed to a legislated ten-mill limit rather than see adoption of a proposal to submit to the people a constitutional amendment limiting millage to ten mills, which if passed by referendum would have been much more permanent than a legislative limit, subject to reversal by any subsequent legislature.[13]

Both Constans and the FEA leadership saw treachery in millage limits. Announcing that "the gun is cocked," Constans anticipated a walkout at a rollback falling below twelve mills because all the special session would accomplish was ad valorem tax relief. When the bill passed anyway, Constans railed against what he called a scheme of putting in money at the state level only to roll back an estimated $82,000,000 at the local level. Observing that acceptance of the legislation would merely prolong the day of reckoning, Constans concluded that only a miracle could prevent a teacher walkout.[14]

On February 14, the day the legislature passed the compromise bill, Christian with his financial expert walked to the FEA building to argue and plead with the FEA directors and Constans for the bill's endorsement. During his ninety minute effort he underscored that while the ten-mill limit was reprehensible, the $254,000,000 compromise package raised per-pupil expenditure to $674, twenty-eight dollars more than the amount recommended by the governor's Quality Education Commission; raised the state guaranteed minimum salary for teachers from $4,343 to $5,300; and, depending on the effects of the rollback, raised salaries for experienced teachers one thousand dollars or more. Besides, Christian honestly felt that this bill was the best that could be passed; he feared that the only alternative was no bill and no money for schools. He then warned his listeners that in the event of a strike, as Florida's chief state school officer, he would fully carry out his responsibilities to assure that the schools continued to operate as required by law.[15]

Noting his very cool reception the superintendent decided to appeal directly to the teachers. At a hastily drawn news conference he informed teachers that since the bill provided the greatest single appropriation for

FEA ACTION

HOLD STEADY

By the time you receive this you will have heard all kinds of rumors.
We are confident that long ago you learned to wait until you received
word from us. Hold steady! If the resignations must be activated,
you will receive the word through-the telephone chain. If we must
move, it is vital that we all move together!

STAND BY

At this writing (Wednesday morning, February 14), the situation looks
very grim. Because of the action of the House of Representatives, the
Senate finance bill has been chopped to pieces in conference committee.
At last reading this conference bill was totally unacceptable. Unless
there is an immediate and dramatic change, the prospects are very poor
that the Legislature will even come close to meeting the needs of education. Consideration of quality education programs died some time
ago.

Throughout this session a majority of the Senators, including members
of both parties, have tried desperately to meet the financial needs of
the schools. On the other hand, the House has been obsessed with ad
valorem tax relief. It appears that the legislative outcome of all this
will be disaster. And as if this weren't enough, over the whole mess
hangs the ever-present threat of a Governor's veto. So stand by!

It might be advisable to remove your personal belongings from the school
at the end of this week and stay very near your telephone Saturday and
Sunday.

WE MUST STICK TOGETHER

We have come this far by sticking together, and come what may we must
see this through together. If we fail to stand together, we can forget
forever our dream of quality education.

Don't be concerned about talk of volunteer substitutes, arbitrary resignation procedures, threatened reprisals or legal action.

If we must resign, we will resign together and we will stick together.

Once we have severed our relationship with the school systems of Florida,
our resignations will remain effective come what may until the Legislature
and the Governor have enacted a satisfactory program into law.

Once we have resigned, nothing will cause us to consider reemployment until
an acceptable educational program has been passed and signed into law.

Florida Education communique getting membership ready for a
walkout in case the legislative conference committee drastically
reduced the benefits of the education finance bill while seeking a
compromise between the senate and the house of representatives
during the special session on education.

education in the history of Florida, a walkout would do nothing more than lose public support for the schools. He then affirmed his commitment to keep the schools open, and urged that teachers remain in their class-rooms.[16]

Other high-level state officials also tried to dissuade the teachers. A representative from Polk County who was a school principal received thunderous applause from his fellow legislators for saying that if the FEA did not accept the legislation he would resign his FEA board position. Several members of the state Cabinet echoed Christian's position warning that they would cooperate in any effort to keep the schools open and would view mass resignations as an illegal strike against the State of Florida. With support from the entire Cabinet, Kirk made arrangements to obtain court injunctions from each circuit court as well as one from the State Supreme Court to stop FEA officials from sustaining a teacher walkout.[17]

Refusing to be accommodated or intimidated, the FEA Executive Committee made thirty to thirty-five thousand resignations effective for February 29, the following Monday. This action started striking teachers toward twenty-one regional centers where the FEA hoped to hold daily meetings to sustain teacher morale while guarding against intimidation and rumor. Breaking the news to the public, Constans described teachers as "sick to death of being blamed for raising the people's taxes" when most of the money would never get to the schools.[18] Estimating tax collection from the special session legislation at $315,000,000, the FEA deleted as not expediting the K through 12 program: $77,000,000 for the ten-mill rollback; $46,000,000 for deficit financing; $43,000,000 for colleges, universities, and vocational schools; $32,000,000 for textbooks and retirement matching, and $4,500,000 for such sundries as hyacinth-growth control and fire ant control and raises for highway patrolmen, leaving a final balance for operating a K through 12 program of $126,233,122.[19] Such duplicity, Constans noted, was sufficient for the FEA Executive Committee to let loose what he described as their "angry tigers," who had already "shoved" the legislature back into session once and planned to do it again in the nation's first statewide teacher strike, depicted by one Cabinet officer as Florida's "biggest crisis . . . since the Civil War."[20]

Chapter Four
Teachers on Strike

AMIDST Constans's claims of school closings, mass meetings, and traffic jams allegedly caused by thirty-five thousand defiant teachers, Christian emerged as the leading force for keeping the schools operational. Christian, who has since related that under some conditions he might have condoned a walkout, disagreed with the current strike. He considered the FEA's actions a betrayal of himself, his staff, and the legislature that had "fought" so hard for a compromise bill. Noting that the compromise if signed into law by Kirk would yield $998,000,000 in total funds for the schools, almost doubling the amount spent during any year in Florida's history and bringing the state to an estimated fourth place in the nation for average teacher salaries, Christian suspected that the NEA might have pushed its Florida subsidiary into a strike as a show of strength in order to end defections to the AFT. Under the circumstances, Christian predicted of the FEA efforts to close the schools, "no one wins and everyone loses."[1]

Indeed, Christian's pledge to keep Florida's schools open dominated his every action. After a strategy meeting with county superintendents at which he announced emergency plans to recruit up to thirty thousand substitutes, the superintendent on February

10, the second day of the strike, secured from the state Cabinet authorization for local school boards to suspend certification standards when hiring substitutes and to release state funds to help pay additional substitutes. Consulting with state attorneys, Christian lent his name to a suit charging the FEA with an illegal strike which

This cartoon warned that if the Florida Education Association's "mass resignation" succeeded powerful public employee unions would soon be dictating to elected officials.

secured a temporary injunction from a Tallahassee circuit court enjoining the FEA from encouraging teachers to continue the walkout. With information from county superintendents, Christian directed that the Department of Education report daily to the news media the number of teachers actually off the job. These statistics, which indicated that the number of participating teachers peaked at 25,712 (nearly 40 percent of Flordia's 58,812 teachers) on the strike's second day, often conflicted with information from the FEA. On the strike's first day FEA communiques claimed 10,200 more teachers absent than did the Department of Education. And throughout the ordeal Constans made claims of more and more teachers abandoning their schools. Against angry blasts of denial from the FEA, Christian announced on the fourth day that over twelve hundred teachers had returned to work and that forty-six of sixty-seven counties had all schools open. At his frequent news conferences analyzing these data, the superintendent offered to meet with any person or group interested in resolving the crisis.[2]

Initially the FEA ignored his offer in favor of negotiating with the governor and the legislature. Kirk's often repeated statement that the legislature "knows jolly well that they better let the people vote [on new taxes for education] or they would get a veto," induced Constans to believe such a veto might force another special session during which striking teachers could secure passage of the Senate appropriations bill. Further encouraging hope, Kirk on a political tour in the western U. S. telephoned Constans and afterwards claimed agreement with the FEA.[3]

The situation became clouded, however, when Kirk, ending a pre-dawn conference with Constans in Tallahassee on February 10, vowed that "the people will control education in the state, not unions." Although what actually was said at this meeting remains in dispute, since then Constans has published a letter depicting Kirk as accepting an offer that if the FEA would issue a return-to-work recommendation to teachers, the governor would veto the legislative package preparatory to calling another special session on education and would announce the compromise himself at a February 21 rally of five thousand striking teachers

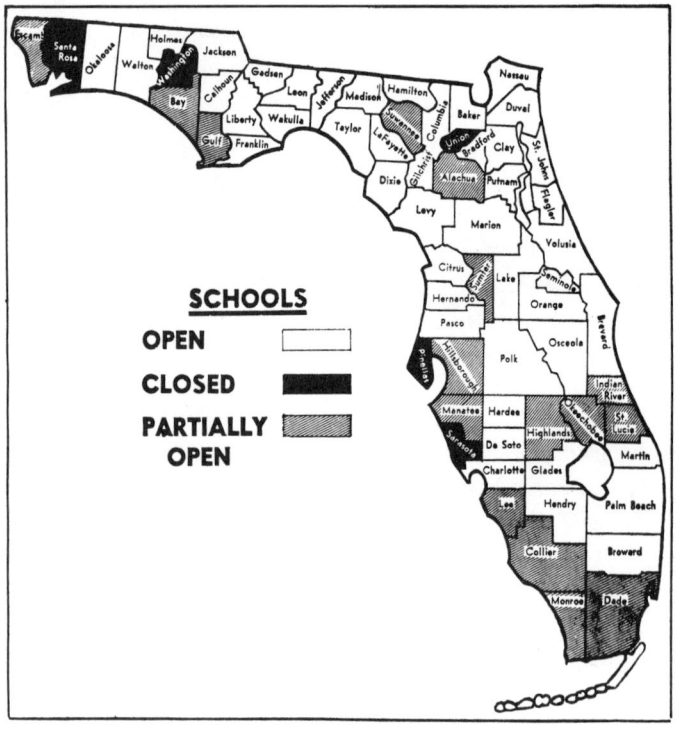

A diagram of the state showing the effects of the walkout based on data from the Department of Education.

in Dade County's Marine Stadium. According to Constans, however, even Kirk's aides became upset when the governor, after a helicopter landing on the stadium field, substituted for his planned speech mere clowning remarks like, "How about a good boo for your governor?" or "How about a hiss then?" Finally the teachers broke their stoney-faced silence with shouts for the governor to get down to business. Under scrutiny of national television, Kirk read statements that "no one is going to coerce me into calling a special session." After this event the FEA never again claimed progress with the governor.[4]

Constans did little better with legislative leaders. Still in session when the FEA called the strike, lawmakers of both parties, reacting angrily to what they considered blackmail, refused all FEA offers to negotiate. Fred Schultz prepared to resign rather "than go back to Tallahassee and change what we have done." Instead they joined Christian and House Speaker Ralph Turlington in efforts to show that the compromise bill did make available for K through 12 education at least $39,000,000 more than claimed by the FEA. Early in the strike this opposition came to a confrontation when the superintendent, two well-known state senators, and several television newsmen made Constans look like "a country boy" on Tampa television programs. Hit by scathing criticism that the FEA had purposely twisted known facts about the funding bill and had misled its membership, Constans admittedly made a "jumbled, incompetent, and unconvincing defense."[5]

In desperation Constans turned to Christian for aid. Incredible as it may seem, Constans says that deep resentment had built up among members of his faction since before the 1967 Legislature, when they felt Christian considered their half billion dollar education program unrealistic and ridiculous. Although Christian, with help from Henderson, had maneuvered through the 1967 session a substantial teacher pay raise bill, Constans has described himself and FEA officials as freezing the state superintendent out of negotiations and activities: "Any time we were in the driver's seat ... we tended to ignore him."[6]

Now, however, with thousands of teachers returning to work in what Constans termed the "drift back," FEA militants were no longer in the driver's seat. As Christian had predicted, teachers made reluctant strikers; a few sent Constans telegrams demanding their resignations back and imploring him to accept Christian's legislative compromise. Among those that did strike there were reports of teachers choked with emotion over leaving their pupils.[7]

Several factors intensified these feelings. In strategically important Broward County where teachers had closed the schools in early September 1967, a court order enforced from that date kept practically all of the county's four thousand teachers on the job. The other sixty-six county school boards encouraged by court injunctions and by state money to pay substitutes made herculean efforts to keep the schools open. In rural counties, school boards promptly accepted resignations, in effect dismissing teachers on strike. In more populous counties where the largest percentages of teachers went out, school boards delayed actions on resignations but raised the pay of substitutes and hired anyone with at least a high school education to staff the schools.[8]

Indeed, teachers felt most disheartened by the angry reaction of the press and public. Already antagonized by teacher actions depreciating the state's national image, Floridians openly denounced teachers for rejecting what most people judged a generous legislative compromise. Moreover, living in a state with a labor force notoriously difficult to organize, Floridians not only had little sympathy with strikes in general, but particularly disliked the spectacle of teachers using this tactic to dictate their salaries to the people's representatives on school boards and in the legislature.[9]

The newspaper coverage best illustrates the prevailing antiteacher attitude. Typically, news reports emphasized

This illustration seeks to point out that teachers fooled no one by brandishing the term resignation to cover an action with all the attributes of a strike.

even the slightest degree of progress in defeating the strike while they played down parental frustrations, school disruptions, and the danger of unqualified substitute teachers causing loss of accreditation for Florida schools. Spurred on by this type of news coverage as well as by editorials, television announcements, and radio addresses that pictured striking teachers as "AWOL" for immorally breaking their contracts and contrasted them with dutiful teachers who stayed with their pupils, thousands of Floridians from every walk of life, even a few legislators, left their daily routine to staff classrooms sometimes at considerable economic sacrifice.[10]

Barraged by CTA pleas to stop the public's classroom walk-in from destroying morale, the FEA communication and publicity system strained in vain to change public opinion. Although willing to spend considerable money, alledged news blackouts in the Tampa area and

'Scab!'

Picketing teachers only interested in more money denouncing a child for crossing their picket line to attend school.

recalcitrant television managers in the Miami area, who denied advertising time, made it almost impossible for the FEA and CTAs to get the teachers' message across about their walkout being a crusade for the good of the children. Instead, all that the public appears to have heard were teacher demands for more salary when they had just received an excellent raise. As the strike progressed, teachers despaired of making Floridians believe that they were engaged in more than a salary grab.[11]

Being isolated, teachers had to maintain their solidarity. For times when they could not personally be with the teachers, FEA leaders used a complicated telephone system to monitor hundreds of meetings and to inform teachers of each other's progress. However, this became increasingly difficult when hostile civic groups forced teachers to change their meeting places, giving rise to communications gaps filled with chilling rumors of young male teachers losing their draft deferments, of a cross being burned on a teacher's lawn, and of teachers receiving harassing phone calls.[12] By far the most damaging rumor, believed even by some high-level FEA officials, had the Dade County Teachers Association issuing a return-to-work order without consulting FEA headquarters.[13] This CTA, which had told teachers of the strike call well before Constans's official announcement and had sent its representatives to address teacher rallies throughout the state, best symbolized teacher resolve. Its president, Janet Dean, and executive secretary, Pat Tornillo, had withstood arrests and jail sentences to lead thousands of teachers at daily rallies in Marine Stadium.[14]

These frustrations culminated in near financial disaster. With hardly any money contributed by outside agencies, teachers had to depend on their meager savings and very small strike funds to maintain themselves.

Adding to the problem angry businessmen called in teacher loans and refused teachers extensions on their bill payments. To keep each other going, teachers shared food, kept their lights off, and formed car pools for even the most routine errands. With morale ebbing very low the NEA sent in field workers to visit teacher groups and help with negotiations, but these workers sent back such discouraging reports that Constans had to empty the FEA treasury before the parent organization would release two million dollars in promised aid.[15]

Still little education went on. Hearing reports of one-third of the schools closed, five hundred thousand children untaught, and of some schools kept open at the price of "near bedlam," principals, parents, and the attorney general began to call on Christian to recommend a statewide school shutdown.[16] Considering such a decision an abdication of duty, Christian toured hard-hit school systems, held emergency mettings with superintendents and directed six staff members to advise local officials on keeping the schools operational. For him, teachers that "honored their contracts," people who substituted in schools, and school boards that kept the schools open were "heroic."[17]

On February 26, when a thousand teachers went back to work in a single day making a total of nearly three thousand returnees since the strike's beginning, Christian began negotiations for a compromise that would end this strike and any possibility of another such confrontation. Preferring professional organizations to unions, he wanted to save the FEA as a significant lobby, but not with sufficient power to run the school system. During conferences strike leaders expressed willingness to modify their original stand, to keep teachers out forever, even if it meant going to jail, unless the legislature gave them the original Senate school funding bill, a professional negotiations statute, a professional practices board, and an improved tenure act.[18]

After a day and night of intense discussion, an agreement was reached. The FEA would call the teachers back to work if the state Board of Education would release $10,200,000 in budget holdback funds, establish a professional standards board, require compliance by counties with the Civil Rights Law, encourage the return of teachers to their old positions without reprisals, and if not offer them assistance from the Department of Education in finding comparable employment. But perhaps most significant for teachers, the state Board of Education would establish procedures for the uniform resolution of grievances by state employees and employ state Deparment of Education staff, "who upon request of county boards of public instruction or certified public school employees will assist in the mutual development and establishment of negotiation procedures." These provisions reflected Christian's belief that the teacher strike had been caused by a communication gap in which teachers were prevented from bringing grievances before their school boards for fair and equitable hearings.[19]

As Christian prepared to present the pact to the state Board of Education, strong opposition developed. At his request on February 28, school board members and superintendents from six large counties with fifteen thousand striking teachers urged the governor to sign the special session education bill and accept the agreement. Kirk, however, resentful at not being consulted on the agreement, called Christian into his office and the two men began shouting when Kirk accused Christian of recognizing the FEA as a union with bargaining powers. At a press conference the next morning, Kirk repeated these charges and threatened a veto if the superintendent and other Cabinet officers did not cease their illegal "secret negotiations." Referring to discontented teachers, Kirk concluded, "let them leave Florida." In a voice choked with anger, Christian told newsmen that unlike the governor he had no interest in running for vice-president, but had "only interest in the welfare of the boys and girls in Florida." Even if the state could hold out for a year, the superintendent

When this cartoon appeared Kirk had just sabotaged Christian's efforts to attain a compromise that would have ended the walkout and reopened the schools.

understood that in too many cases "we are not teaching school but merely keeping school."[20]

The following morning Christian presented his compromise to the state Board of Education. After exchanging several verbal raps with the governor, Christian declared that refusal to take some action would literally destroy Florida's public school system. Yet with the attorney general running as a conservative for the U.S. Senate and opposing Christian's agreement as fostering professional negotiations, the decisive vote on the five-man board rested with the state treasurer. About to make a reelection bid, this official cited telephone calls and telegrams "about 100 to 1 against the compromise" and voted with the secretary of state and the attorney general for a postponement until March 4.[21]

After this setback, many county school boards and their superintendents joined those opposing Christian's compromise. Late in the evening of February 29 the Duval County School Board led many county school boards and the state School Board Association to condemn the proposed settlement as "surrender of control of public schools to the teachers' union." Christian, stubbornly searching for support, met with a group of two hundred county school board members and county superintendents to explain his proposal. He reported that over three thousand telegrams had been received from distraught parents; one of the best put it succinctly, "Do something, damn it; my children are not in school." Nevertheless, many of those present denounced his compromise for guaranteeing professional negotiations and for forcing local boards to take back striking teachers. Noting a division of opinion, Christian cancelled the March 4 state Board of Education meeting.[22]

With displeasure Christian read Constans's statement: "We've heard the reports on the attitudes of school board members and will never crawl back into their schools." Constans's resentment had reached a high point because after cheering teachers with news of an imminent settlement he had been forced less than two days later to tell them that the Cabinet had squashed their hopes.[23]

The fortunes of the militant teachers took a decisive downturn when the legislative package became law without Kirk's signature on March 7, prompting many teachers to return to work. Most of these teachers felt that the prospects for another special session had become hopeless when Kirk refused to exercise his veto powers. Constans, ignoring several restraining orders, took over the telephone system to get CTA leaders to keep their teachers off the job only to be told that teachers were returning anyway because of complications with their pension and tenure status.[24]

Unaware that Constans had lost control of his membership and still hoping to secure an honorable settlement to save the integrity of the FEA, Christian reconvened the state Board of Education to try once more for a compromise settlement. On March 8 the board adopted a measure that, while providing for release of $10,200,000 in budget holdback funds, mentioned neither professional negotiations nor compliance with the Civil Rights Act, but instead stipulated that the final authority for setting minimum education standards and employing teachers, including those that had resigned, rested by law with county school boards. A dejected Constans turned over responsibility for announcing the end of the strike to Hagman, who stated that "because we believe our achievements . . . are significant enough that our teachers can return to their schools with heads held high . . . and have placed service above self, the executive committee of the FEA therefore recommends that all teachers who resigned return to their schools on Monday."[25]

Christian immediately organized a task force of three high-level staff members and eight field consultants to negotiate with school boards on rehiring teachers without prejudice by classifying their absences as professional leave. Invariably, Kirk undermined his efforts by charging that Christian fraternized with the teachers' union and by advocating that school boards take a tough line to show teachers that they must never again strike against the State of Florida.[26]

As had happened previously many school boards agreed with the governor. In Broward County the school board, at emotionally charged hearings, fired seventy-one teachers for participating in the walkout, some with over twenty years' experience; in Lee County returning teachers paid hundred dollar fines to obtain reemployment at the status of beginning teachers. In thirty-six other counties involving 4,130 teachers the impasse dragged on sometimes for weeks with school boards locking out teachers, firing principals implicated in the strike, and circulating blacklists of strike leaders. In almost every county striking administrators were demoted to teachers and striking teachers lost their tenure rights, returning to work at the pay of beginning teachers. According to one source, seven thousand teachers were displaced, three thousand of them leaving the state.[27]

Christian and his task force strenuously fought against these conditions. When invited either by a school board or a CTA, they spent many hours before lively audiences advocating the return of teachers. Meeting stubborn resistance, Christian telephoned county superintendents and school board members to arrange personally for the reassignment of teachers. He also brought to the Department of Education several talented principals fired as a consequence of the strike.[28]

Despite the superintendent's efforts, Constans would not lift statewide sanctions while reprisals continued against teachers. In fact, Constans tried several times to restart the strike by reminding teachers of their share in the pledge: "No one goes back until we all go back." Rejected on the home front, Constans sent truth squads of striking teachers to speak throughout the nation on the inequities in Florida.[29]

Christian did not agree with Constans's attitude. Since the strike was lost, Christian counseled that teachers should do everything in their power to rebuild Florida's state and national image. Only by such means could the gains of the 1968 Legislature be sustained. He especially resented Constans's acting in bad faith because the Department of Education rehiring efforts had fulfilled the state's part of the negotiated agreement, and he expected Constans to follow by lifting statewide sanctions. Unknown to Constans, at one point Christian contemplated court action against the FEA. Finally, in August 1968 the FEA Board of Directors voted to lift statewide sanctions.[30]

The defeat of the teachers left a large void in the pattern of state school leadership. Had the FEA accepted the legislative compromise, attributed by practically everyone to the zeal displayed by organized teachers, it is possible that Floridians would have recognized a new Christian-Constans school lobby. But this possibility ended when the FEA emerged from the strike with heavy losses in membership, with a nearly bankrupt treasury, and with an image so distorted that beginning in 1969 a newly elected board of directors purged all FEA officers including Constans that had masterminded the strike.[31]

Chapter Five
Threshold of a New Era

THE STATE legislature, filling the leadership void left by the eclipse of the Florida Education Association, brought Florida education to the threshold of a new era with a statewide comprehensive plan to encompass both learning objectives and equitable funding formulas. If the ultimate trauma of teachers by the thousands rebelling against the state could be traced to a single glaring deficiency it had to be that Florida for too long had depended on a crisis-to-crisis syndrome for running the school system. Back in 1967, while events rushed toward confrontation, the legislature had recognized the need for total planning in education and for assessing the performance of supervisory, administrative, and instructional staff. The 1968 special session went further specifically directing the chief state school officer to expand the capability of the Department of Education for effecting constructive educational change and for providing and coordinating the creative services necessary to achieve greater quality and efficiency in education.[1]

By enacting the Education Improvement Expense Fund (EIEF) the legislature took an early tentative step toward giving county school boards broad responsibilities for determining how state funds should be spent to bolster local school programs. Unprecedented in Florida history, this act required counties to submit plans for educational improvement to the state school superintendent in order to receive their share of the plan's fourteen million dollar allocation.[2]

Events, however, moved too rapidly for these innovations to prevent the teacher strike which so depreciated public faith that new directions became more imperative than ever. Floridians speaking out claimed to have lost their innocence regarding the dedication of teachers after witnessing them abandon their classrooms to force more salary money from the state. Some of the most bitter of these critics, citing the testimony of laymen substitutes during the strike, expressed a conviction that anyone could do a better job with the schools than the educators.[3]

Determined after this shocking altercation to strengthen Florida government and rebuild the credibility of public education, the legislators reassembled on June 24 for constitutional revision. Among their most important achievements was to provide for annual sessions of the legislature and governmental reorganization. Regarding education, the legislature gave a vote of confidence to Florida public school leaders by calling for placement of the entire school system under an elected chief state school officer, titled the commissioner, responsible to an elected Cabinet State Board of Education. By this action, the lawmakers nullified an act passed at the special session directing that the people vote on an amendment removing the elected superintendent from the constitution.[4]

Immediately after ratification of the new constitution, House Speaker Fred Schultz in a pace-setting speech to the organization session of the House on November 12, 1968, announced three formidable challenges to be met by the 1969 reorganization session: (1) creation of a new management system to cope with the growing complexities of government; (2) forming a new approach to education; and (3) becoming a more active and responsive legislature. The Speaker visualized five years to institute a planning-programming-budgeting system to replace government by intuition with government by logic. Already Schultz had received much approval for his speeches on the subject given before the House and before audiences throughout the state. He traced the beginning of the process to the 1967 Legislature which had created the Office of State Planning and made the auditor responsible to the legislature rather than the executive. The key, however, for Schultz would be establishment of standing committees, twenty-eight in the House, each with its own staff to develop legislative programs touching every aspect of state government. Schultz wanted a "full-time" legislature that would initiate state programs and policies rather than one that, as in the past, just reviewed for passage proposals drawn mainly by state Cabinet officers and their staffs.

Of special concern to Schultz was a more effective school system. The Speaker believed that "in education we stand on the brink of the most important changes ever experienced in this field." According to him the basic structure of education involving a teacher, a textbook, and a classroom could no longer meet the needs of Florida's fast-moving and affluent society. Aware that education was resistive to change, he wanted the legislature to make strong efforts to develop a system of schooling emphasizing modern technology to produce discernible learning results.[5]

The 1969 session consummated many of these ideas. Organized under the new constitution along the lines described by Schultz, the Florida legislature, costing the taxpayer $9,300,000 annually, was considered the nation's fourth most effective legislative system. The representatives planned to use this system to scrutinize every aspect of government as a basis for making broad policy decisions.[6]

The Government Reorganization Act of 1969 made appointive officials subordinate to elected ones. At the top of the state education system, the legislature placed the people as represented by their elected representatives. Executive authority for carrying out legislated policies issued from the Cabinet State Board of Education which in turn relied on the commissioner to set and implement with executive approval supervisory and administrative procedures for school programs. The commissioner presided over all aspects of state-supported education including the university system, which hitherto had answered only to the legislature. That those carrying on the executive function would be most effective in their roles, the legislature required them to divest themselves of as much administrative trivia as possible to concentrate on study, research, evaluation, overall coordination, and policy decisions.[7]

After restructuring the school system, the lawmakers sustained the progress of innovative planning. Establishing a new lawmaking concept of "plan now and finance later," the legislature placed at the disposal of the commissioner eighty-four thousand dollars to plan a Research and Development Program (R & D) with the promise that if the resulting scheme proved acceptable, implementation funds would be forthcoming from the next legislature. Presented as an education program unique to Florida, R & D incorporated a procedure common in private industry of making available developmental capital to high-level management for planning purposes.[8]

Perceiving that Florida was moving toward comprehensive planning and financial equalization in education,

the commissioner on July 29 presented recommendations to the state Board of Education delineating the
roles, under governmental reorganization of the state,
the commissioner, and the Department of Education.
He wanted Florida to have statewide educational objectives, a strong program of financial support for education, minimum standards of achievement, quality controls, efficient information systems, consultant services
to counties, and most important incentive systems for
influencing counties to go beyond a minimum performance. Christian outlined twelve objectives as the commissioner's role centering on isolation of specific societ-
al needs to be served by education and creation of a
multi-year master plan to ensure attainment of high-
priority objectives. The mission of the Department of
Education, Christian described as "exercising public
responsibility for providing an education that will enable and encourage each citizen to develop his fullest
potential and thus become a maximum contributor to
and beneficiary of a free society."[9]

Soon after the state Board of Education approved his
proposals, the commissioner concentrated on a millage
equalization scheme to supplement the MFP. Six years
previously, Superintendent Bailey had pointed out that
the weighted index of taxpaying ability which determined a county's share of the MFP was continually
rendered obsolete by Florida's rapidly changing economy. Based on sales tax returns, gainfully employed
workers, value of farm products, value of railroad and
telegraph property, and auto tag sales, the index was not
only questionable as to its representativeness but it did
not account for local sources of tax revenue being
limited to ad valorem property taxes. By this system an
estimated twenty-seven counties with high per capita
incomes in 1969 registered high on the tax-raising index

but could not adequately support their schools because of an abundance of low-value farm acreage that offset even twenty-mill levies. Moreover, in the thinking of some legislators high millage levies fell too harshly on a few industries with substantial assessed values.[10]

Representing a county that suffered from all these disabilities, House Speaker Fred Schultz had been adamant in his demand for reform. A major architect of the ten-mill limit, Schultz was also credited during the 1968 session with influencing substitution of a six-mill levy for the index of taxpaying ability in the MFP. During the 1969 session he presided over intense debates which resulted in a bill reducing the local MFP contribution to three mills and requiring a tax ratio study as a basis for redistributing MFP funds held back from counties below 100 percent assessment. Passed over the governor's veto at a special session, this plan still was unable to remedy the injustices of low millage yields.[11]

On August 21 the commissioner outlined to the joint meeting of the Senate and House Education committees a district ad valorem equalization proposal as a remedy. Christian possessed especially strong credentials for developing a workable equalization method. Praised by R. L. Johns, coauthor of the MFP, for his outstanding knowledge of educational finance, Christian had introduced modern systems of budgeting and auditing when he was superintendent of schools in Pinellas County.[12]

The commissioner told the legislators that a study of counties near full value assessment showed a millage yield range per student in average daily attendance from $6.94 in the property poorest county to $76.71 in the property richest county. In the face of the ten-mill limit on local taxation, property poor counties could never achieve programs even approximating those provided by their richer neighbors. As an alternative to such extreme and injurious variations, Christian recommended that the state allocate thirty-two million dollars to supplement budgets of forty-three counties educating 46 percent of the state's school children with millage yields below the state average of $24.00. To foster local initiative, the plan specified withholding for reallocation through the MFP a prorated amount of state funds from counties below 100 percent assessment and below ten mills. The commissioner at all hazards wanted to keep the state-county partnership in balance and to avoid "the simple solution" of total state financing of education leading to state control.[13]

There followed considerable discussion. Several legislators voiced concern that the plan did not go far enough to ensure equality. Because the so-called penalty clause if applied too often would defeat the whole purpose of the plan, one legislator suggested distribution of thirty-two million dollars through the MFP. Conversely, a colleague from one of the more urbanized counties condemned this approach because he perceived the MFP as "an elaborate set of formulae to hide this whole business of sharing with the poor" and also condemned the Christian approach because of the impossibility of determining 100 percent assessment. As a substitute he proposed a flat amount for each student from the state to be adjusted lower if districts did not measure up to accreditation standards. Other urban county legislators opted for an index, adjusting tax yields with differentials in living costs, a factor attenuating even the highest tax yields in some heavily populated parts of the state. In general, legislators from comparatively property rich counties with constituents tired of subsidizing their poorer neighbors requested a plan that would benefit every county.

The commissioner made a spirited defense of his plan. In no way did Christian believe he had found a solution to all the evils of financing state government; but at least his plan guaranteed a minimum millage yield, giving children some semblance of equal opportunity. At the same time, he considered it necessary that some differences remain between counties so as not to interfere with local initiative, the foundation of any excellent school program. Nor did he want to become a "regular czar" that set accreditation standards for determining which counties received state money. Instead Christian proposed releasing money in such a way as to rectify obvious inequities and enable counties to set their own priorities in spending the funds rather than be limited to the standardized constraints of the MFP.[14]

The 1970 session demonstrated the salutary effects of a closer working relationship between the legislature and the Department of Education. In consideration of the commissioner's ideas and the questions raised by urban county legislators, the lawmakers incorporated in the MFP a one-mill yearly increase in the amount of local contributions to the level of seven mills together with an eleven hundred dollar yearly state increase per current expense unit till 1972. Beginning in 1974, the state would distribute revenue through the MFP to reflect local changes in the cost of living. That counties burdened with low millage yields should be able to upgrade particularly deficient aspects of their school program, the Christian Plan was to operate until counties reached the seven-mill limit in 1972.[15]

A history-making session in the field of educational finance, the 1970 Legislature also started the state toward accountability in education. Legislation required the commissioner to prepare a procedural plan by March 1, 1971, objectively assessing progress in education to involve uniform evaluation in each school district respecting predetermined objectives and using measurement tools that accounted for national trends. In support of this orientation the legislature provided

$1,200,000 for R & D projects endorsed by the Department of Education dealing with performance assessment and goal clarification. Appraising the work of the legislature throughout the period of crisis, the commissioner noted a turning point in public education toward comprehensive planning, funding equalization, and accountability.[16]

Chapter Six

A New Era

I N THE 1970s these trends accelerated into a strategy for keeping the legacies of strained federal-state
relations, student unrest, and partisan politics from
plunging the schools to another nadir of public confidence. After the epic struggles of the late 1950s, no
further legislative movements interfered with Bailey's
and then Christian's policy of reasonable compliance
with ceaseless Federal demands for more and more
school desegregation. In 1967 when the percentage of
children attending school with at least some members of
the other race rose sharply from 43 percent to 65
percent, Florida was cited by a high-level federal official
as having the best record for desegregation in the
southeast and as good a record as any border state. In
the realm of federal aid, Christian, perceiving an opportunity for educators to do things that they had only
dreamed of, advocated that the state obtain as many
grants as possible, a policy which helped generate 9
percent of Florida's school budget in Washington.

Upsetting the often fragile balance of federal-state
relations, the Supreme Court in October 1969 named
Florida as one of the states affected by its drastic
decision that complete desegregation be accomplished
immediately. Subsequent lower court rulings imperiling

federal funds, and directives from federal agencies requiring burdensome cross bussing to achieve racial balance, which would disrupt the schools at mid term, in
1970 brought the patience of Floridians near the breaking point. Governor Kirk aggravated the situation by
threatening to suspend school officials and to hold back
state funds of school districts complying with court
ordered bussing. Lending credence to his threat, the
governor took over the Manatee County school system
in April 1970 with sixty state officers to resist federal
marshals for a week in a futile attempt to prevent cross
bussing.

Reacting to the challenge Christian chose a moderate
course. He sought to obtain more reasonable desegregation deadlines from the courts while preventing the
governor from causing defiance of federal law. In pur-
suit of this dual policy, Christian secured authorization
from the state Board of Education for its attorney, an
experienced civil rights lawyer, to write briefs that
eventually helped gain postponements for many counties "in agony" over desegregation deadlines. Appalled
at Governor Kirk's attempts at intimidation of county
school personnel, the commissioner promised to use his
official powers to prevent any such misuse of executive
authority. On speaking tours of the most troubled areas,
the commissioner received enthusiastic applause for his
stand in favor of reasonable compliance and his plea for
Floridians to remain calm and to obey the law so that
relations between the races would not be drastically set
back.[1]

In the midst of this altercation the perennial genera-
tion gap amplified by the Zeitgeist of upheaval also had
a detractive effect on the public's attitude toward the
schools. As if the national scandal of long-haired youth
defying the values of their parents in street demonstra-
tions and general radical behavior had not shaken

Floridians enough, these phenomena becoming apparent at Florida schools had erupted in the late spring of 1970 and again in 1971 into major confrontations at the state's oldest university. "Why spend my hard-earned money to educate a bunch of long-hairs who want to destroy me?" was a typical complaint too often heard by the commissioner.[2]

Alienated from a school system apparently producing little more than militant teachers, rebellious youth, and racial incidents, Floridians seemed ready to embrace schemes for radically transforming the public schools or even substituting an alternative means of education. Particularly noteworthy to Florida educators because of its simplicity and because of its apparent return of control of education to the people was a plan for distributing tax dollars as vouchers or educredits to be used by parents for purchasing their children's education at the public or private school of their choice. Abetting the possibility of this in Florida was the growing number of parents paying hundreds or even thousands of dollars annually for private school education, emphasizing a sense of community, academic achievement, low teacher-student ratios, and religious training. Another popular scheme reaching outside the traditional relationships of public education was performance contracting, already being tried out in Duval County. By this scheme, school boards contract with private firms, typically paying for services only after an agreed upon amount of learning has been demonstrated by the students.[3]

As controversy raged, Reubin Askew stepped into the governorship. His victory over Kirk, after a five-week whirlwind campaign, indicated that Floridians had chosen reasoned and deliberative leadership to heal scars left by the explosive 1960s. Their school systems experiencing frequent disruptions, their cities bursting with people, their waterways and air turning fetid with pollution, their woodlands and coastal lands being gobbled up by developers, Floridians had begun to question the belief so prevalent in the '60s that the highest possible rate of population and industrial growth alone ensured prosperity for their state. Aware of the change, aspirants for the governorship had centered their campaign on how to make life better for those now residing in the state. Of course the question of taxes as the key to any change in the role of government became the main issue of the campaign. And Kirk's consumer tax record proved no match for Askew's demand that wealthy industries pay their share of the cost of improving Florida through a corporate profits tax and a more extensive severance tax. Conveying an attractive wholesomeness, Askew seemed ready to use lessons learned during twelve years in the legislature to end government by special interests in Florida.[4]

Still, relatively unknown outside of his legislative district until he challenged Kirk, Askew remained a bit of an enigma. Concerning education policy, his most frequently quoted remark, spoken as part of his inaugural address, was "to accomplish reform in the education system." When pressed for more detail he answered that educational change would have to await resolution of the state's financial woes. Christian, however, had known Askew as a member of the House Appropriations Committee, the select committee on post high school education, and Schultz's bipartisan committee on the education crisis to be a "friend of education."[5]

As Askew would have it the issue of the corporate profits tax took precedence over other considerations. Having repudiated the politics of no new taxes, Floridians were falling victim to its legacy. A financial crisis which had already dissipated a $63,500,000 surplus with five months left in the fiscal year threatened a deficit as high as $250,000,000 just to maintain current levels of state services during the next fiscal year. Corporate profit tax promoters inundated the state with accounts of how a tax rate equalling twenty-seven cents per thousand dollars of corporate income in Florida, second lowest rate among fifty states and $6.24 below the national average rate, had resulted in such extreme inelasticity, regressiveness, and unfairness in the tax system that if tax reform was not forthcoming a fiscal crisis could be expected every few years.[6]

Among all state dependent services no agency suffered more from financial reverses than did education. With the school system already burdened by a 1 percent holdback in state funds costing twenty-three million dollars, and anticipating another one-half percent holdback, the commissioner asked county school boards for a return of capital outlay funds to prevent cuts in the MFP. A report issued by the Senate Ways and Means Committee showed that to keep pace with Florida's population growth it would take $104,000,000 in additional funds during the next fiscal year just to maintain present levels of education.[7]

In spite of all these factors, and educators fanning out across the state soliciting citizen support, the legislators dealt the corporate profits tax a disheartening setback. Illustrating his needs at the special session, Askew reported a 6 to 1 Supreme Court advisory opinion that a constitutional amendment would be necessary for such a levy. He especially wanted to obtain a two-thirds vote from the legislature for getting an amendment on the ballot in April so that the hundred million dollars in expected revenue from a corporate profits tax could be distributed to hard-pressed agencies at the earliest possible date. Although seemingly a sound proposition, GOP representatives marshalled by the House minority leader

attacked the idea of any new taxes before state government had been made efficient and current state taxes
had been rid of inequities. As debate on the merits of
new taxes versus austerity filled the legislative halls, the
sixteen leading lobbyists in what Askew liked to call
Florida's shadow government wielded incalculable but
considerable influence. Weighted in favor of industrial
and business interests, the resources of Florida's shadow
government largely helped the Republicans kill the
governor's early vote scheme, seeming to keep a corporate profits tax amendment off the ballot until November 1972.[8]

Disappointed with the work of the special session, the
commissioner blamed the state's financial dilemma on a
few legislators who might have given the business community a year of grace but had done so at the expense
of the boys and girls of the state. He also expressed
resentment at the legislature's refusal to postpone implementation of a plan initiated in 1969 calling for with-
holding of MFP funds from counties below 100 percent
assessment as determined by a tax ratio study. Because
of this setback, Christian estimated that thirty school
districts would have to cut teacher salaries and other
aspects of their program to meet assessment penalties.[9]

Described as "hard charging and high paid," legislators were looking beyond the special session for ways to
get better results from education. At conferences
around the state a troop of House Education Committee
members organized by Committee Chairman Terrell
Sessums recoiled when educators detailed Florida's low
national ranking for educational appropriations. Hurling
terms like differential staffing, accountability, assessment, and performance contracting, these legislators
wanted learning outcomes emphasized rather than expenditures. Sessums even went so far as to employ

graduate student researchers who told a convention of county superintendents at Gainesville that the legislature ought to scare "you guys" into action by trying out the voucher plan because with a monopoly on the market educators had drowned a lot of ideas in bureaucratic decadence.

When given their chance, the educators came right back with the weaknesses of the school system. One superintendent found the problem in his principals whose poor training set a low tone for the schools; another blamed oversized bullies causing frequent disruptions. Everyone agreed on the major adjustment problems caused by lightning-paced school desegregation.[10]

The lawmakers, however, were in step with national trends. To countervail buck-passing in public education, legislatures across the nation had begun seeking means to inform the public of progress toward achieving maximum returns in educational outcomes for tax money spent on public education. The NEA, surveying the nation, detected this movement in thirty states.[11]

Informing his colleagues of attitudes in Florida, Sessums described the legislature as under the gun to provide means for showing specific learning outcomes from the large expenditures on instruction. He told the House Appropriations Committee that too often schools functioned as little more than baby-sitting endeavors or as a means of fighting unemployment. Responding to Sessums, a high-level Department of Education official suggested a way out of the rut was objective testing by grade level to find the weaknesses in the system and then the development of a statewide strategy to correct deficiencies.[12]

On March 24, 1971, Christian presented to the House Subcommittee on Appropriations his department's plan for educational assessment. Defining accountability as the process of explaining the utilization of resources in terms of their contribution to desired results, the plan stipulated a three-phase operation extending over a five- to seven-year period. Phase 1, to begin in the 1971-1972 school year, involved isolation of desired outcomes and monitoring discrepancies between pupil performance and those outcomes. With the exception of assessment in reading and certain occupational areas, assessment would begin in the elementary level and in succeeding years move through the high school. That this would not be just a blind acceptance of existing educational priorities, the first phase would involve an impact assessment of the relevance of in-school learning experiences to the social adjustment requirements of the learner. Operational assessment would involve criterion-referenced tests measuring student achievement against stated performance objectives and norm-referenced tests measuring student achievement against that of a representative sample group. A decision to concentrate first on reading in all grades was based on the assumption that the vast majority of educational activities depended on reading skills, that Florida youth performed below the national norm on reading tests, and that assessment techniques in the area were in an advanced state.

Occurring simultaneously with this procedure would be Phase 2—Cost Analysis. The model chosen by the department would provide cost data on use of resources in relation to stated outcomes. Of special importance was separating cost and noncost factors such as disposition of persons toward the task, managerial know-how, technological factors, and so forth. Information gleaned from these two phases would form the basis for Phase 3—Process Assessment, which meant analysis of educational procedures in terms of their efficiency in producing desired learning in students. Given that industrial models of assessment were not considered easily transposed to educational models, the Department of Education would initially concentrate on appropriate model development for application of the phase by 1972. The result of this phase it was thought would be better awareness of the most efficient combination of methods, media, and grouping for a school course to achieve stated objectives.[13]

To obtain backing for the program, Christian told the committee that widespread loss of confidence in the public schools was the abiding concern behind the movement for educational accountability. Whether it could be traced to poverty, ghetto patterns, discrimination, or whatever, he found the people tired of education being the dinosaur of American society. As an alternative, he proposed that educators strike out boldly by making themselves accountable to the people for contributing to a free and open, compassionate society that is nonracist, multicultural, and productive. For an accountable educational system to become a reality, Christian believed that educators must transform their view of the school system from a time-based orientation to a performance-based orientation emphasizing student growth. Such a change further requires that the focus of assessment be adjusted. Learning outcomes should be measured not so much against individual students' performance on undependable teacher-made tests as on their measured learning discernible from carefully drawn tests standardized for specifically structured educational programs.[14]

The legislature overwhelmingly passed the Department of Education plan as the Eduational Accountability Act of 1971. The law requires that by November 1, 1972, and each year thereafter the commissioner, with approval from the state Board of Education, establish specific uniform statewide educational objectives for each grade level including but not limited to reading, writing, and mathematics. To attain these objectives, the law specifies that the commissioner as well as each district school board make progress reports on the new strategy regarding the schools within their jurisdiction. Their reports are to include assessment results gained from criterion-referenced tests and norm-referenced tests by grade and subject area with analysis and recommendations concerning the cost differential effectiveness of instructional programs. Consistent with this policy, the commissioner was to prepare by the 1973-1974 school year accreditation standards based upon a school's progress toward educational objectives. The law's implementation schedule further directs that assessment for reading should be operational by the 1971-1972 school year and for writing and mathematics by the 1972-1973 school year. By this act, the lawmakers hoped the major concern of state-level leadership in eduation would be improving the learning performances of every child in relation to stated educational outcomes.[15]

This legislature nevertheless proved more receptive to planning than to funding. Affected by the slow pace of educational change and the antieducation feelings sweeping the state, the lawmakers gave way to partisan issues when funding most phases of education. South Florida representatives spawned a movement to take their ten-county area from the jurisdiction of the Department of Education on the grounds that a regional office staffed by the counties would better serve the area's needs. Able to head off this action as a threat to statewide comprehensive planning, the commissioner found himself the brunt of scathing criticism that the property assessment penalty clause of the "Christian Millage Equalization Plan" unduly made school children pay for wrongs perpetrated by county tax assessors. Christian added to his previous request for suspension of the clause a request that the ten-mill limit be lifted temporarily to give districts adjustment time, but representatives from counties especially profiting from the reallocated money caused rejection of the proposal. Breaking into these discussions were anti-intellectual comments fostered by the image of the universities as a disruptive force in society. These issues, converging with the need to justify a seventy-five million dollar severance tax levy as not going for wasteful school programs, persuaded the lawmakers to fund only half the 1970 legislative equalization plan, to terminate the Christian plan altogether, and to underfinance the universities, colleges, junior colleges, and vocational education programs. For Christian, this meant that in just one year the legislature had shifted its priorities away from education.[16]

Undismayed, the commissioner kept morale high among his staff. As perceived by Christian the role of the Department of Education "team" was to keep the legislature abreast of ideas propelling the state toward a comprehensively planned school system capable of engendering the highest possible amount of learning in Florida's 1,400,000 school children. Department of Education staff despite intermediate setbacks became increasingly encouraged by the genuine commitment to education of the governor and powerful members of the legislature.

Askew, beginning in the summer of 1971, showed himself a stalwart in helping the citizenry understand the importance of racially balancing the schools to build a more democratic society. With Christian reminding Floridians that since blacks for decades had endured unjustifiable bussing to perpetuate a segregated school system it was only fair that Floridians endure hardships necessary to integrate the schools; Askew added the supportive reason that to be rid of racial bussing, Floridians must fully integrate their society. Such strong support from the governor inspired confidence in state education officials that the 1972 Legislature would yield a good human relations program.[17]

In the meantime the governor's education committee of twenty-two citizens from all walks of life studied the educational system from top to bottom to determine needed improvements. Under the guardianship of Chairman Fred Schultz, the committee was to derive from recommendations made by experts representing the Department of Education, the universities, and private industry a master plan for directing the future of Florida education. Enhancing the success of the venture, representatives from both legislative chambers acted as members of the governor's committee while heading parallel studies of the school system.[18]

Still there remained significant differences on how best to improve public education. Using an interim report from the citizens' committee as his basis, Askew strongly supported by House Education Committee Chairman Terrell Sessums and House Speaker Richard Pettigrew opened the 1972 Legislature with a drive to get a constitutional amendment on the ballot empowering the governor with Senate approval to appoint the state Board of Education which in turn would appoint a commissioner of education. Taking this plan under advisement, the commissioner conceded that the obligations of the Cabinet to the public school system perhaps should be transferred to an appointed school board, but continued to disagree that the choice of the state chief school officer should be taken from the people. Fomenting a campaign with the help of present and former Cabinet members to retain an elected commissioner, Christian felt gratified when Pettigrew withdrew the proposal after, by a very narrow margin, it fell short for a second time of the seventy-two votes necessary for approval by three-fifths of the House.[19]

This discordant note silenced, another sounded over the bussing issue. The same political faction that had opposed the governor over the corporate profits tax and was finally turned around by public pressure to pass it

during a special session in 1971 took advantage of
statewide antibussing agitation to get a straw ballot on
the question of an antibussing amendment to the U.S.

'Them? Oh, They're Grownups'

Children of both races portrayed as mature enough to accept
integration if their parents would stop the foolish protesting over
busing.

Constitution. Askew's supporters immediately intervened to add a countervailing question on equal educational opportunity. As expected, On March 14, 1972, with busses rolling for racial balance in every school district, Floridians voted in favor of equal educational opportunity for all but overwhelmingly against cross bussing to attain it.[20]

Politics subsiding, the legislature achieved important precedents for financial equalization and comprehensive planning. Overcoming the equalization setback of the previous session, the legislature passed an additional allotment of $1,650 per expense unit and a differential cost-of-living allotment to districts accompanied by a 1.5 mill increase in the local required MFP effort. Combining the new fiscal policy with the commitment to comprehensive planning, this law also required that each school district develop and apply a model for comprehensive educational planning as a qualification for participation in the funding program. According to subsequent Department of Education guidelines these plans should include: "(1) A clear statement of philosophy. (2) Goals which are consistent with the State goals for education and the philosophy and policies of the district school board. (3) Both annual and long-range (five-year) objectives which are consistent with district goals and are based on assessed needs. (4)An evaluation design for measuring progress toward achieving specific objectives."[21]

While it is difficult to document, it is probable that nationally publicized breaks with educational tradition favorably affected the pace of educational change in Florida. Regarding funding equalization, for example, a California high court had shocked Americans by declaring the state's property tax invalid for fostering unconstitutionally wide discrepancies between the quality of education offered in property rich and property poor districts. Discussing this case with an assemblage of school board members, Florida's commissioner praised the 1972 Legislature for contributing to a degree of funding equalization that would meet any constitutional test.[22]

The lawmakers during the 1973 session combined a revolutionary concept in state funding equalization with the highest possible levels of local initiative for comprehensive planning as the Florida strategy to improve public education. Following the recommendations of the Governor's Committee on Education, the lawmakers replaced the MFP with the Florida Education Finance Program (FEFP). This program accounts for each district's number of full-time students, type of instructional programs, cost-of-living factors, and millage yields to attain a level of equalization in Florida surpassing every state but Hawaii and guaranteeing "every public school student (K–12) programs and services appropriate to his educational needs, which are substantially equal to those available to any similar student regardless of geographic location or local economic factors."[23]

Important for district-level planning, the new fiscal arrangement specifies a maximum of flexibility. In place of the MFP's dependence on instructional units and average daily attendance as distribution factors, the FEFP incorporates a formulation based on full-time equivalent students (FTEs) into its distribution index. More than just a reflection of the number of public school students registered in a district's schools, FTEs are weighted in terms of the kind of programs students are involved in, yielding values as low as unity (1 FTE) for a student in basic programs of grades 1 through 12 and as high as fifteen (15 FTEs) for a student in some exceptional education programs. Promoting flexibility in staffing procedures, the new law transfers to the districts responsibility for employing supervisory personnel, for setting teaching load guidelines, and for setting minimum salaries at each instructional rank. These latter provisions combined with a statute requiring district school boards to arrange, insofar as practicable, incentives for self-improvement and efficient service should enable district-level planners to relate competency of school personnel to educational goals.[24]

Such a progressive fiscal policy enhances the legislated intent that the Florida strategy for comprehensive planning be a two-way process involving decentralization of the decision-making process and accountability for learning outcomes. To gain the broadest possible public endorsement, state and local agencies are collaborating to establish educational goals and to assess educational progress in consultation with almost every part of Florida society. This commitment is particularly evident in a law effective for the 1973-1974 school year requiring district school boards as the major planning unit to examine closely information and recommendations contained in annual evaluations of school progress made by one or more school advisory councils; these councils are to be broadly representative of the community but must include both parents and students.[25]

Also implicit in this law is a policy that the school be the unit of accountability. Reporting to a convention of secondary principals, Commissioner Christian announced that the law will act as a principal's report card by letting the public know how well the students of a given school are doing, how well the teachers are doing, and how well the principal is doing in improving the school. In the commissioner's view, this reflects the well-documented maxim that the success of a local school depends in the final analysis on the effectiveness of the school principal. Laws of this type along with the state's increasing emphasis on school accreditation standards based on the validity of instructional procedures and student performance, it is hoped, will bring the decision-making process closer to the learner, where it is considered to be most effective for giving Floridians the highest possible educational return for their tax dollars.[26]

Coordinating these policies throughout the state is the responsibility of the Department of Education under the overall supervision of the commissioner of education. In keeping with the 1971 Accountability Act, the Department of Education through its various research and development programs is continually creating, refining, and applying assessment tools for the state while inculcating awareness of the new approach in the public through workshops, training programs, and brochures. With enactment of the mandate for district-level planning in 1972, the Department of Education has been engaged in an intense effort to provide local units with information, consultant resources, and in-service training programs vital for effective planning and innovation. So that the state could be particularly efficient in providing these services, the legislature in 1973 required the Department of Education to consult with state university education deans on setting up teacher centers deploying university professors to strategic locations throughout the state for in-service training and consultant services. A major interpreter of the Florida strategy for comprehensive planning and accountability, the associate commissioner of education for planning and coordination describes the state as striving to achieve the following goals in public eduction: (1) greater responsibility on the part of local school districts for education; (2) greater emphasis on school-based decision-making; (3) comprehensive planning; (4) eliminating excessively restrictive statutes and state board regulations; (5) greater emphasis on performance-based education; (6) encouraging alternatives in education; (7) explaining the utilization of resources in terms of their

contributions to the attainment of desired results (accountability). Essentially, then, Florida's educational
leaders seem to be striving for a well-planned and
well-managed school district-based educational system
capable of setting and achieving educational goals with a
maximum of flexibility and efficiency.[27]

The enactment of far-reaching programs for funding
equalization and comprehensive planning indicates that
Florida once more has a committed coalition for better
education dominated by high-level state officers. Addressing an institute of state superintendents at Hyannis
Port, Massachusetts, soon after legislative adjournment
in 1973, the commissioner described the governor, the
legislature, and the chief state school officer, together
with their staffs, as Florida's team for better education.
Preparing the game plan for the team, Florida legislators
have relied not merely on information gathered specifically for their use by their own staffs, the Department
of Education, and executive agencies of government;
they have also had available data provided by the FEA
and by hundreds of prominent citizens participating as
part of councils, commissions, and associations both in
and out of government. Once the legislature has assimi-
lated the information into a school program, budgets
prepared separately by the governor's fiscal advisors and
the state Board of Education are reviewed by the
legislature to ensure that the final education budget
places the financial needs of education in perspective
with those of all phases of state government.

Still, there remain areas of healthy disagreement
which keep Florida's leaders alert to the needs of
education. Aggressive legislators and their often young
and idealistic aides sometimes have pushed so hard that
the lines between the executive and legislative branches
of government have become blurred by legislation directing the commissioner not only in what programs

must be achieved but also in how and when to execute them. Abhorring any such concentration of power, Christian gave notice of readiness to protect the system of electing the commissioner to retain the checks and balances inherent in a system that includes a chief state school officer with executive authority independent of both the governor and the legislature.[28]

Florida has traveled a rocky road from an education coalition dependent on the charismatic leadership of Tom Bailey and Ed Henderson to one embracing most of the leaders of state government. Sounding the death knell for the first coalition was a legislature burdened by low pay, long adjournments, and an unrepresentative apportionment formula precluding in but a few of its members sufficient knowledge of education to prevent the schools from being sacrificed to special interests, economic austerity, narrow prejudices, and chaotic politics. Spreading this pattern to the executive branch, three successive governors adopted programs more reflective of partisan issues than of good education. Bailey and Henderson battling hard against these tendencies achieved some remarkable programs but lacked sufficient support to prevent factionalism from erupting into the state's gravest crisis in public education.

The resulting years of confrontation politics pointed up some of the school system's most glaring deficiencies. Governor Kirk, for all his polemics and bellicose gestures on behalf of taking over the schools did much to muster support for more efficiency and planning in education. Likewise, Constans and the thousands of teachers that backed him illustrated a need not only for more equitable salaries, but also for more teacher involvement in the decision-making process and a more equal funding formula. Although eventually beaten back, these factions proved to be the ultimate adversaries, threatening to take from the people's elected authorities control of the school system if the authorities did not come up with more effective ways to accomplish educational objectives.

Striving to turn crisis to progress, the commissioner and his staff seized on incidents of teacher militancy, racial disruptions, and youthful rebellion to stoke the drive for a better funded and a better planned school system. As public frustration with the schools intensified, state educators found increasing support for their plans among the people's representatives in the legislature. Indeed, it was the people, sobered by the disruptions of the '60s, who ratified a constitution calling for more efficient state government and elected a governor committed to making that government accountable to the people. Those changes set the groundwork for a new era in Florida education.

Today the destiny of Florida education is in the hands of the people's elected officers, all of whom have shown commitment to a better school system. The legislature, made among the most efficient in the nation by governmental reorganization, has been joined by the governor in a deep commitment to a well-financed and well-planned school system that is accountable to the people. Moreover, as designated by the tenets of republican democracy, no officer has ultimate power over the schools but instead power is diffused throughout the state and local governments to best protect the people's interests. That this system of checks and balances will not degenerate into factionalism, inhibiting educational progress, officials from state and local government are united in a persistent effort to apply a comprehensive plan for education capable of inspiring confidence in the great majority of Floridians.

Notes

Chapter 1. Roots of Crisis

1. Interview with Thomas D. Bailey, Tallahassee, December 11, 1972 (Library of Oral History, University of Florida, Gainesville).
2. Radio script, Kenneth Ballinger interviewing Thomas D. Bailey, September 1950, Crisis in Education File (Office of Communications and Media Services, State Department of Education, Tallahassee, Florida, hereinafter cited as OCMS).
3. Interview with Thomas D. Bailey, Tallahassee, August 6, 1973.
4. Ibid.; interview with Ed B. Henderson, Tallahassee, August 15, 1972 (Library of Oral History, University of Florida, Gainesville); *Jacksonville Chronicle*, November 1, 1957.
5. *Jacksonville Chronicle*, November 1, 1957.
6. Thomas D. Bailey to Select Committee of the House of Representatives "Index of Taxpaying Ability" (March 18, 1963) in 1963 Legislative Summaries Files (Office of Public Information Services, State Department of Education, Tallahassee, Florida, hereinafter cited as OPIS); Bailey, "A Report: Florida Schools," *Florida School Bulletin* 22 (June 1960): 5; Bailey, "Will Florida Keep Pace with Space in Education?" *Trails in Florida Education* (Tallahassee, 1963), p. 234.
7. *Jacksonville Florida Times-Union*, June 12 and 30, 1957; *St. Petersburg Times*, June 30, 1957; interview with Howard J. Friedman, September 12, 1973; *Ocala Star Banner*, June 9, 1957.
8. Helen L. Jacobstein, *The Segregation Factor in the Florida*

Democratic Gubernatorial Primary of 1956 (Gainesville: University Presses of Florida, 1972), pp. 19-21; Donald D. Chipman, The Development of the Florida State System of Public Education 1922-1948 (Ph.D. diss., Florida State University, 1971), p. 118; *Journal of the House of Representatives, State of Florida Thirty-Sixth Regular Session . . . 1957* (Tallahassee, 1957), pp. 12-13.

9. *Miami News*, May 19, 1957; *Gainesville Sun*, June 9, 1957; Floyd T. Christian, *Message to the 1971 Legislature*, p. 5, Legislative 1971 File, OPIS; *Jacksonville Florida Times-Union*, June 30, 1957.

10. Howard J. Friedman, Legislative Memo No. 10 (June 10, 1957), Legislative 1957 File, OPIS; Friedman, Summary of 1957 Legislative Action Pertaining to Education (June 24, 1957), ibid.; interview with Ed Henderson, August 15, 1972, *St. Petersburg Times*, February 17, 1965; LeRoy Collins, speech, November 6, 1958, in Desegregation 1958 File, OCMS.

11. Department of Education-Florida Education Association (hereinafter cited as DOE and FEA), *Summary of 1959 Legislative Action Pertaining to Education*, Bulletin No. 11 (June 29, 1959), pp. 1, 36-37; *Jacksonville Florida Times-Union*, June 19, 1959; *St. Petersburg Independent*, June 19, 1959.

12. Facts concerning the percentage of general revenue funds allocated to schools can be found in the *Florida School Bulletin*, title changed to *Florida Schools* in 1966, published by the DOE; also see *Miami Herald*, February 22, 1968.

13. *Orlando Star*, June 1, 1955; *Panama City Herald*, June 1, 1955; *Miami Times*, June 4, 1955; *Tallahassee Democrat*, February 16, 1956; Jacobstein, *Segregation Factor*, pp. 70-71; L. L. Fabisinski, et al., A Report of the Special Committee, July 16, 1956 (OPIS); *Miami Daily News*, July 22, 1956; *Deland Sun-News*, July 29, 1956; *Tallahassee Democrat*, July 31, 1956.

14. First used in a *Tampa Tribune* editorial in 1955 to describe specifically the actions of a Senate clique in blocking reapportionment. The term "Pork Chop Gang" crept into the vocabulary of Floridians in the 1950s and 1960s, when it was said that legislative apportionment was based more on pine trees than on people; see Allen Morris, comp., *The Florida Handbook, 1973-1974* (Tallahassee: Peninsular Publishing Company, 1973), p. 150.

15. That the governor and legislature clashed over this issue indicated the undemocratic character of Florida government. Although Collins had been the first Florida governor to win over 50 percent of the popular vote in the Democratic primary, his Democratic legislature contained a majority of rural county representatives from counties that had voted large majorities for his segregationist opponents. Jacobstein, *Segregation Factor*, pp. 70-71.

16. *1955-1966: Journal of the House of Representatives Extraordinary Session . . .* 1956 (Tallahassee, 1956), pp. 154, 177. An account of this adjournment episode is in Jacobstein, *Segregation Factor*, p. 74.

17. *Tampa Morning Tribune*, August 2, 1956; *Tallahassee Democrat*, August 16, 1956; *Melbourne News*, June 7, 1956; *Pensacola Journal*, June 8, 1956; Jacobstein, *Segregation Factor*, p. 74; *Journal of the House of Representatives, State of Florida Thirty-Sixth Regular Session . . .* 1957 (Tallahassee, 1957), pp. 12-13.

18. *Tampa Tribune*, October 2, 1956; *Tallahassee Democrat*, October 7, 1957; *Jacksonville Florida Times-Union*, October 13, 1957; *Jacksonville Chronicle*, November 1, 1957.

19. *Journal of the House of Representatives, State of Florida Thirty-Seventh Regular Session . . .* 1959 (Tallahassee, 1959), p. 23; DOE-FEA, *Summary of 1959 Legislature*, p. 8. In September, 1959, Dade County attempted to desegregate an elementary school, but only fourteen whites were enrolled among several hundred students. Jacobstein, *Segregation Factor*, p. 75.

20. DOE-FEA, *Summary of 1959 Legislature*, pp. 1, 36-37; *Jacksonville Florida Times-Union*, June 19, 1959; *St. Petersburg Independent*, June 19, 1959.

21. *St. Petersburg Independent*, June 19, 1959; James L. Wattenbarger, "A Report: Junior College Opportunities," *Florida School Bulletin* 22 (September, 1960): 19; *Kissimee Gazette*, September 28, 1967.

22. DOE-FEA, *Summary of 1959 Legislature*, pp. 36-37; *St. Petersburg Independent* June 5, 1959; *St. Petersburg Times*, June 7, 1959; *Jacksonville Florida Times-Union*, June 13, 1959.

23. *Tampa Morning Tribune*, May 9, 1959; Thomas D. Bailey, "Remarks Before House Committee on Public Education and Higher Education" (May 8, 1959), Textbook File, OPIS; *Ocala Star Banner*, May 8, 20, 1959; *Deland Sun-News* May

14, 1959; *Jacksonville Florida Times-Union*, May 16, 1959; *Tallahassee Democrat*, May 26, 1959.

24. Undated resolution with memo from the Governor's Office, June 12, 1959, in Howard J. Friedman, Personal File, OPIS; *Miami Herald*, June 7, 1959; *Jacksonville Florida Times-Union*, June 13, 19, 1959; *Tampa Tribune*, June 17, 19, 28, 1959; *Daytona Evening News*, June 19, 1959; *Bradenton Herald*, June 21, 1959; *Ocala Star Banner*, June 22, 1959; *St. Petersburg Times*, June 10, 1959.

25. NEA, *Florida: A Study of Political Atmosphere As It Affects Public Education* (Washington, D.C., 1966), pp. 61-62; *Miami Herald*, May 23, 1971.

26. *Tampa Tribune*, April 5, 1961.

27. DOE-FEA, *Analysis of Education Legislation, Special Release* (June 23, 1961). It was stongly suspected that the requirements for teachers to make a score of 500 on the NTE was particularly aimed at black teachers who were beginning to enjoy advantages under federally induced school desegregation. In 1963, for example, estimates had 81 percent of the black teachers taking the examination scoring below the legal minimum compared to 34 percent of the white teachers. J. T. Campbell, Projects to Upgrade Preparation of Teachers, November 8, 1965, Desegregation 1965-1966 File, OCMS.

28. *Tallahassee Democrat*, June 1, 1961; DOE-FEA, *Legislative Summary*, No. 9 (June 2, 1961); DOE-FEA, *Analysis of Education Legislation, Special Release* (June 23, 1961), p. 9.

29. DOE-FEA, *Analysis of Education Legislation, Special Release* (June 23, 1961), p. 9; Thomas D. Bailey, Statement, July 27, 1961, with Report of the Florida Legislature Investigation Committee to the 1961 Legislature, 1961 Legislative Summary File, OPIS. In 1963 the Florida Supreme Court ordered reinstatement of three teachers who had been fired because of the committee's allegations of homosexual practices; in doing so the court cited the committee for acting beyond its authority. *Orlando Sentinel*, March 30, 1963.

30. *Daytona Beach Evening News*, April 11, 1961; see also Textbook General File, OCMS.

31. Thomas D. Bailey to Select Committee of the House of Representatives, "Financing of the Minimum Foundation Program," March 18, 1963, Legislative Summary File, 1963.

32. Thomas D. Bailey to Select Committee of the House of Representatives "The State's Purchase of Textbooks," March 18, 1963, Legislative Summary File, 1963, OPIS.

33. Farris Bryant, *The Message of Governor Farris Bryant to the 1963 Florida Legislature* (Tallahassee, 1963), pp. 3-4, 6, 8-9; FEA, *Legislative Bulletin,* No. 10 (May 31, 1963), p. 10.

34. *St. Petersburg Times,* February 27, 1965; *Orlando Dispatch,* undated clipping in C.W.G. to Howard J. Friedman, October 13, 1963, in Textbook General File, OCMS; Hillel Black, "What Our Children Read," in Glenn Smith and Charles K. Kniker, *Myth and Reality: A Reader in Education Foundations* (Boston: Allyn and Bacon, 1972), p. 92.

35. *Miami News,* April 25, 1964; *Orlando Sentinel,* April 25, 1964; *Ft. Lauderdale Daily News,* April 25, 1964; *Tallahassee Democrat,* January 20, 1965; *West Palm Beach Post,* January 21, 1965; *Orlando Sentinel,* January 21, 1965.

36. Haydon Burns, *Message to the 1965 Legislature April 6, 1965* (Tallahassee, 1965).

37. FEA, *Legislative Bulletin* No. 1 (April 9, 1965), pp. 1-4; *Miami News,* April 8, 1965.

38. Miami News, *February 14, April 8, 1965; Orlando Sentinel,* June 6, 1965; *Political Atmosphere,* p. 13; *Tampa Tribune,* June 16, 1965.

39. FEA, *Legislative Bulletin,* No. 9 (June 4, 1965), pp. 1-2; *Political Atmosphere,* pp. 22-23; *Jacksonville Florida Times-Union,* June 1, 1965; *Collier County News,* June 10, 1965; *Orlando Sentinel,* June 21, 1965. Political atmosphere was defined as "the state of affairs which is shaped by influences, controls, powers, decisions of individuals and groups in the government of public schools." *Political Atmosphere,* p. 3.

40. Thomas D. Bailey, "Will Florida Keep Pace," p. 234; James Cass, "The Florida Story: Politics and Education in the Sunshine State," *Saturday Review* (April 20, 1968), pp. 162-163; Arthur O. White, "The Man in the Middle: Floyd Christian and Florida's Crisis in Education" (DOE, 1973); *Political Atmosphere,* pp. 2-3.

41. Cass, "Politics and Education," pp. 62-68; *Political Atmosphere,* p. 27; "Walkout in Florida," *Time* 91 (March 1, 1968): 70-71; *Tampa Tribune,* June 13, 1965, September 10, 23, 1967; *Titusville Star Advocate,* September 21, 1967; Gayle Norton, "The Florida Story," *Phi Delta Kappan* 49 (June 1968): 557.

42. Allen Morris, comp., *The Florida Handbook, 1971-1972* (Tallahassee: Peninsular Publishing Company, 1971), pp. 60-61, 130-131; Cass, "Politics and Education," p. 65; *Orlando Sentinel,* April 14, 1961; *Deland Sun-News,* April 30,

1961; Park B. Loren, Ira A. England, "Florida Education Running a Political Obstacle Course," *Phi Delta Kappan* 50 (September 1968): 27-33; David Halberstam, "Claude Kirk and the Politics of Promotion," *Harper's* 238 (May, 1968): 39.

43. Cass, "Politics and Education," p. 65. In noting this expenditure an article in *Harper's* attributed the absence of direct money payoffs to the fact that legislators "cut from the same cloth" as lobbyists, routinely passed bills favoring the special interests. These interests were identified as the citrus, livestock, and farming interests, private power and transportation interests, labor industry, retail merchants, municipalities, insurance groups and the landowners, bank owners, and growers of pine trees. Robert Sherrill, "Florida's Legislature: The Pork Chop State of Mind," *Harper's* 231 (November 1965) cited in *Political Atmosphere*, p. 44.

44. Christian, Message to 1971 Legislature, p. 5; *Pensacola Journal*, April 16, 1961; *St. Petersburg Independent*, June 12, 1959; *Tampa Tribune*, April 27, 1969; Thomas D. Bailey, Statement, May 3, 1961, 1961 Legislative Summary Files, OPIS.

45. Bailey, *Trails in Florida Education*, p. 234; Floyd T. Christian, *Reaching for Greatness*, February 24, 1966 (Tallahassee, 1966); Christian, *Golden Opportunities Address to the FEA*, Miami, April 22, 1966, OPIS; *Miami Herald*, September 10, 1967; *,Lakeland Ledger*, September 12, 1967; *Political Atmosphere*, p. 122.

46. *Political Atmosphere*, pp. 26-28.

47. Headlines of newspapers accounting legislative reaction in May 1965, reprinted in *Tampa Tribune-Times*, October 1, 1967; *Orlando Sentinel*, June 2, 6, 1965; *Tampa Tribune*, June 3, 1965; *Daytona Beach Morning Journal*, June 12, 1965.

48. *Deland Sun-News*, June 3, 1965; *Tampa Tribune*, June 10, 1965; *Political Atmosphere*, p. 1; *Arcadian*, June 10, 1965; *Miami Herald*, June 10, 1965; *Tampa Times*, June 11, 13, 1956; *Plant City Courier*, June 17, 1965; *Pensacola News*, July 30, 1965; *Miami News*, September 19, 1965.

Chapter 2. Gaining a Truce

1. Arthur O. White, interview with Floyd T. Christian, May 21, 1973, DOE; *Biographical Data—Floyd T. Christian Commis-*

sioner of Education, State of Florida, September 9, 1971, Office of the Commissioner, Tallahassee; *Orlando Sentinel,* October 17, 1965; *St. Petersburg Times,* October 30, 1965; *Ft. Pierce News Tribune,* October 31, 1965; *Gainesville Daily Sun,* October 31, 1965; *Tallahassee Democrat,* November 3, 20, 1965, January 31, March 5, 1966; *Miami News,* February 6, 1966; *St. Petersburg Independent,* June 12, 1959.

2. *St. Petersburg Times,* October 30, 1965; *Orlando Sentinel,* December 19, 1965; *Jacksonville Journal,* October 18, 1967; *Pensacola News,* November 3, 1965.

3. Floyd T. Christian, Address to Florida School Board Association and FEA Department of County Superintendents, November 29, 1965; Christian, Address to Leon County Lions Club, January 6, 1966. During the first month of his administration, Christian gave at least 28 addresses all over Florida on these themes; see Floyd T. Christian Speeches, 1965-1966 File, OPIS.

4. *Deland Sun-News,* November 7, 1965; Floyd T. Christian, *Reaching for Greatness* (Tallahassee, 1966).

5. Replies to those making congratulations are found in "Reaching for Greatness"–Governor's Conference on Education File, OCMS; *Winter Haven Daily News Chief,* February 27, 1966; *Clearwater Sun,* February 27, 1966; *St. Petersburg Independent,* June 12, 1959; *Daytona Beach Evening News,* April 1, 3, 1961; *Tampa Tribune,* April 11, 1961; *Daytona Beach Evening News,* March 11, 1965; *St. Petersburg Times,* October 12, 1965, January 30, 1966; *Miami Herald,* October 13, 1965; *Tallahassee Democrat,* January 31, March 5, 1966; *Miami News,* February 6, 1966.

6. *Winter Haven Daily News Chief,* February 27, 1966; *Clearwater Sun,* February 27, 1966.

7. *Florida Education* 43 (March 1966); *Political Atmosphere,* pp. 2, 192; *Tampa Tribune,* March 21, 1966. The report, *A Study of Political Atmosphere* consists of 198 pages of statistics, appendixes, and statements pointing out Florida's deteriorating education situation. Secreatry of State Tom Adams after reading the report was amazed "that the 1965 Legislature appropriated 1 percent less proportionally from general revenue than was allocated in the 1963 session." *Florida Education* 43: 2.

8. *Tallahassee Democrat,* March 11, 1966.

9. Ibid.; *Tampa Tribune,* March 21, 1966; *Bradenton Herald,* September 8, 1967.

10. *Pensacola News*, November 3, 1965; *Biographical Data—Floyd T. Christian*; Floyd T. Christian, undated speech in NEA Investigation File, OCMS.

11. *Jacksonville Florida Times-Union*, June 10, 1965.

12. *Claude Kirk's Position on Education* (Ft. Lauderdale, 1966), Claude Kirk File, OCMS, pp. 11, 12, 18; *Daytona Beach Evening News*, December 14, 1966.

13. *Tampa Tribune*, June 4, 1965; Morris, *Florida Handbook, 1972–1973*, pp. 128-131; *Political Atmosphere*.

14. *Orlando Sentinel*, October 3, 1967; *Tallahassee Democrat*, September 16, 1967.

15. *St. Petersburg Times*, October 1, 1967; interview with Ed Henderson, August 15, 1973.

16. Loren and England, "Political Obstacle Course," pp. 27-33; *Political Atmosphere*, p. 59; Halberstam, "Politics of Promotion," pp. 33-40.

17. *St. Petersburg Times*, February 22, September 3, 1967; Halberstam, "Politics of Promotion," pp. 33-40; *Tampa Tribune*, January 2, 1967.

18. *Gainesville Daily Sun*, April 26, 1967.

19. Ibid.; *Vero Beach Press Journal*, May 4, 1967.

20. *Tampa Tribune*, October 4, 1967; *St. Petersburg Times*, September 6, 1967; *Miami Herald*, October 1, 1967.

21. FEA *Legislative Report* No. 4, *April 38, 1967; Jacksonville Florida Times-Union*, September 3, 1967; *Miami Herald*, September 7, 1967; *St. Petersburg Times*, May 8, 1967; *Jacksonville Journal*, May 17, 1967; Floyd T. Christian, Statement, April 27, 1967, in notebook of Al Erxleben (DOE); White, Henderson interview, August 15, 1972; FEA, *Legislative Report*, Nos. 8, 15, May 26, July 18, 1967; *Orlando Sentinel*, June 4, 1967.

22. Manning J. Dauer, "Florida: The Different State," in William C. Havard, ed., *The Changing Politics of the South* (Baton Rouge: Louisiana State University Press, 1972), p. 123; Events Prior to the 1968 Teacher Walkout and Chronology, unpublished paper, Crisis News Release File, OCMS. According to Senate President Verle Pope, "Florida will spend $3 per pupil less for basic education needs in 1967-1969 than in the past two years." *Miami Herald*, September 7, 1967.

23. *St. Petersburg Times*, October 15, 1967.

24. Ibid., September 20, 1967; interview with Ed Henderson, August 15, 1972; interview with Floyd Christian, May 7, 21, 1973; *Tampa Tribune*, July 14, 1959; *St. Petersburg Times*,

February 11, 1968.

25. *Lakeland Ledger*, September 12, 1967; *St. Petersburg Times*, September 20, 1967.

26. FEA, *Legislative Report*, Nos. 10, 13, 15, June 9, 30, July 18, 1968.

27. Ibid.; *Orlando Sentinel*, June 4, 1967; *Tampa Tribune*, June 7, 1967; *Miami Herald*, October 1, 1967.

28. *Miami Herald*, October 1, 1967; *Walkout in Florida*, pp. 70-71; *St. Petersburg Times*, October 15, 1967.

29. FEA *Action*, July 18, 1967; Phil Constans to Cliff Cormier, January 31, 1973, in *Gainesville Daily Sun*, February 18, 1973. Every spot in the stadium must have been filled because the seating capacity has been estimated at 17,000 to 20,000 people. *Jacksonville Florida Times-Union*, November 20, 1973, and *Tampa Tribune*, November 22, 1973.

30. *Miami News*, August 26, 1967; *St. Petersburg Times*, September 20, 1967; *Miami Herald*, October 2, 1967; *Titusville Star Advocate*, October 10, 1967; *Tampa Tribune*, September 24, 1967; Cocoa *Today*, October 19, 1967; *Hollywood Sun Tattler*, September 26, 1967; Constans to Cormier, January 31, 1973; *Miami Herald*, October 4, 1967.

31. *Miami Herald*, October 4, 1967; *St. Petersburg Times*, October 15, 1967; *Miami Herald*, September 21, 1967.

32. *Lakeland Ledger*, September 9, 20, 1967; *Miami Herald*, September 21, 1967.

33. *Miami Herald*, October 10, 1967; Constans to Cormier, January 31, 1973.

34. *Miami Herald*, September 20, 23, 1967.

35. *Lakeland Ledger*, September 12, 1967; *Miami Herald*, September 14, 1967; *Miami Herald*, September 26, 1967; untitled analysis of Kirk's speech with rebuttals in Crisis Governor Kirk File, OCMS.

36. Analysis of Kirk's speech.

37. *Ft. Lauderdale Daily News*, September 8, 1967; *Orlando Star*, September 8, 16, 1967; Cocoa *Today*, September 9, 1967; *Miami Herald*, September 10, 1967; *Pompano Beach Sun Sentinel*, September 12, 1967; *Cocoa Tribune*, September 13, 1967; *Orlando Sentinel*, September 13, 1967.

38. *Clearwater Sun*, September 10, 1967; *Ft. Lauderdale News and Sun Sentinel*, September 10, 1967; *Ft. Lauderdale Daily News*, September 14, 1967.

39. *Ft. Lauderdale Daily News*, September 14, 1967; *Miami Herald*, October 13, 1967.

40. *Miami Herald*, September 8, 14, 1967; *Ft. Lauderdale Daily News and Sun Sentinel*, September 10, 1967; *Tampa Tribune*, September 10, 1967; *Pompano Beach Sun Sentinel*, September 12, 13, 1967; *Winter Park Sun Herald*, September 14, 1967; *Miami Herald*, September 14, 1967.

41. Newspaper opinion is summarized in the *Miami Herald*, September 11, 1967.

42. *Miami Herald*, September 16, 23, 27, 1967; *Tampa Tribune*, September 20, 1967; *Ft. Lauderdale Daily News*, September 26, 1967; *Miami Beach Sun*, September 17, 1967; *St. Petersburg Times*, September 27, 1967; *Bradenton Herald*, September 28, 1967.

43. *Miami Herald*, October 18, 1967; Arthur O. White, interview with Wade Hopping, May 25, 1973, DOE.

44. *Miami Herald*, September 8, 1967; *Tampa Tribune*, September 23, 1967.

45. *Tampa Tribune*, September 23, 1967.

46. *Jacksonville Florida Times-Union*, October 6, 1967; White, Hopping interview, May 25, 1973; *Tampa Tribune*, September 9, 1967. Christian was often characterized as the "Man in the Middle" while he contended with the various factions; see for example George Hanna, "Christian in with the Lions," Cocoa *Today*, February 28, 1968.

47. *Orlando Sentinel*, September 22, 1967; White, Christian interview, May 21, 1973.

48. *Tampa Tribune*, October 18, 1967; *Daytona Beach Morning Journal* October 3, 1967; *Titusville Star Advocate*, October 10, 1967; *Miami News*, July 7, 1967.

49. *Miami Herald*, September 7, October 3, 1967; unidentified clipping in September, 1967, Crisis File OCMS: Floyd T. Christian, *Address to National Meeting of Superintendents of City County School Systems of 100,000 to 300,000 Students, Winston-Salem, North Carolina, October 18, 1967*, OPIS.

50. Phil Constans, *The Crisis in Education*, September 19, 1967, mimeograph, FEA File, OCMS. That Kirk and Constans could come up with such widely different figures indicated that they had chosen to emphasize different aspects of the financial situation. For example, the governor spoke correctly when he claimed that $.67 of every general revenue dollar went for education, but at the same time failed to mention that general revenue funds accounted for less than half the total expenditures of government. Constans making up for

the governor's oversight came up with another correct but much smaller figure of $.29 of the total revenue dollar. *Miami Herald*, September 26, 1967.

51. Constans, *Crisis in Education*.
52. Floyd T. Christian, *Crisis in Florida Education: A Radio and Television Address, September 19, 1967*, Crisis News Release File, OCMS; *Tampa Tribune*, September 20, 1967; *Tallahassee Democrat*, October 1, 1967.
53. *Miami Herald*, September 21, 1967; Cocoa *Today*, September 27, 1967; *St. Petersburg Times*, September 28, 30, 1967; *Ft. Lauderdale Daily News*, September 29, 1967; *Tallahassee Democrat*, October 1, 2, 1967; *Pensacola Journal*, October 3, 1967; *Miami Herald*, October 2, 1967; *Tampa Tribune*, October 4, 1967.
54. *Tallahassee Democrat*, Ocotber 20, 1967.
55. *Tampa Tribune*, October 15, 1967; *Miami Herald*, October 13, 1967; *Orlando Sentinel*, October 19, 1967; *Tallahassee Democrat*, October 20, 1967.
56. Cocoa *Today*, September 13, 1967; *Orlando Sentinel*, September 13, 1967; *Ft. Lauderdale Daily News*, September 16, 1967; *Miami Herald*, October 13, 1967; *Tallahassee Democrat*, October 20, 1967.
57. Floyd T. Christian, *Sanctions*, Crisis News Release File, OCMS: Christian, *Some Suggestions for Dealing with Mass Resignations of Teachers*, September 6, 1967; ibid.
58. *Tampa Tribune*, October 18, 1967.
59. *Jacksonville Florida Times-Union*, September 23, 1967; *Miami Herald*, October 19, 1967; *St. Petersburg Times*, October 15, 1967; *Tampa Tribune*, October 15, 1967; *Jacksonville Journal*, September 22, 1967; *Tallahassee Democrat*, October 20, 1967.
60. *Miami Herald*, October 19, 1967; *Orlando Sentinel*, October 19, 1967; *Tallahassee Democrat*, October 20, 1967.
61. *West Palm Beach Post*, October 19, 1967.

Chapter 3. A Short Truce

1. *Orlando Sentinel*, October 16, 1967.
2. *Ft. Myers News Press*, October 24, 1967.
3. *St. Petersburg Times*, September 28, 1967; *Tampa Tribune*, September 28, 1967; *Ft. Lauderdale Daily News*, September 28, 1967.

4. *Miami Herald*, September 29, 1967; *Orlando Sentinel*, November 16, 1967.

5. *Orlando Sentinel*, November 19, 20, 1967.

6. *A Report by the Governor's Commission for Quality Education to Governor Claude R. Kirk, Jr.*, December 22, 1967 (Tallahassee, 1967), p. 8.

7. Interview with Floyd T. Christian, May 21, 1973.

8. *Miami News*, February 1, 1968; Floyd T. Christian, *Address by Superintendent Floyd T. Christian to Joint Session of the Legislature, January 31, 1968*, Crisis News Release File OCMS.

9. Arthur O. White, interview with Howard J. Friedman, May 18, 1973, DOE; FEA, *Legislative Report* No. 3, February 9, 1968 (Tallahassee, 1968); Floyd T. Christian, Statement, February 15, 1968, in Special Session 1968 File, OPIS.

10. Eldridge R. Collins and Howard J. Friedman, "The 1968 Special Session Legislature," *Florida Schools*, 30 (March 1968): 14-21; *Tampa Tribune Times*, March 17, 1968.

11. Christian, Statement, February 15, 1968, Crisis News Release File, OCMS; FEA, *Legislative Report* No. 3, February 9, 1968; interview with Howard J. Friedman, May 18, 1973. Assessment increases had frequently been caused by teachers suing in the name of taxpayers. In Duval County suits had increased assessments by 365 percent making possible large teacher salary increments which could be maintained despite a millage rollback. *Tampa Tribune*, June 13, 1965; February 2, 1968; *Miami Herald*, February 16, 1968. The heart of the tax was a 1 percent increase in the sales tax, 20 percent of which would be paid by visitors to the state.

12. *St. Petersburg Times*, February 13, 1968; *Miami Herald*, February 13, 1968. These counties were all well above 12 mills and in the case of Broward County, the people had recently approved 15 mills as part of a 5-year master plan for educational improvement. *Miami Herald*, February 28, 1968.

13. *St. Petersburg Times*, February 13, 1968; *Miami Herald*, February 13, 1968; *Pensacola Journal*, February 23, 1968.

14. *Orlando Star*, February 15, 1968; *Tampa Tribune*, February 15, 1968; *St. Petersburg Times*, February 14, 1968. Senator Lawton Chiles, a Lakeland Democrat who helped write the Senate education package, said a compromise between the education and tax relief forces had become necessary to get any education plan through the legislature and he insisted that the plan still represented a great step forward in education. *Tampa Tribune*, February 15, 1968.

15. Arthur O. White, interview with John Seay, May 19, 1973; White, Christian interview, May 21, 1973; *St. Petersburg Times*, February 15, 1973; *Orlando Sentinel* February 15, 17, 1968; *Lakeland Ledger*, February 16, 1968; *Deland Sun-News*, February 16, 1968; *Daytona Beach Evening News*, February 15, 1968; *Tampa Tribune*, February 15, 1968.

16. *St. Petersburg Times*, February 16, 1968; *Deland Sun-News*, February 16, 1968; *Tallahassee Democrat*, February 17, 1968.

17. *Orlando Sentinel*, February 17, 1968; *Tampa Tribune* February 22, 1968; Norton, "The Florida Story."

18. *St. Petersburg Times*, February 15, 1968; *Tampa Tribune*, February 15, 1968; *Orlando Sentinel*, February 17, 1968.

19. FEA, *Fiscal Facts* in notebook of Al Erxleben, DOE. This was only the beginning of what one irate citizen called the "sick" arithmetic regarding the school finance bill. For example, on the size of the rollback, the state cited figures between $66,700,000 and $69,000,000 while FEA computations ranged from $77,000,000 to $82,000,000. According to Constans one reason for the difference was that the state based its estimates on last year's tax collections while the FEA based its estimates on projected tax revenue for 1968–1969. Ibid.; *Miami Herald*, February 25, 15, 1968; *Tampa Tribune*, February 14, 1968; *Pensacola Journal*, February 23, 1968; *St. Petersburg Times*, February 15, 1968.

20. *St. Petersburg Times*, February 11, 1968; *Tallahassee Democrat*, February 17, 1968; in one dispatch Constans described the teachers as "driven to resign in futility because they cannot secure adequate financing for education in Florida." Constans, statement, February 17, 1968; *Tampa Times*, February 17, 1968.

Chapter 4. Teachers on Strike

1. Constans, Statement, February 19, 1968; *FEA News*, February 19, 1968, Crisis FEA File, OCMS; White, Christian interview, May 21, 1973; *Miami Herald*, February 18, 1968; *Orlando Sentinel*, February 23, 1968; Norton, "The Florida Story," pp. 557–558; Floyd T. Christian, Statement, February 23, 1968, Crisis News Release File, OCMS.

2. *Miami Herald*, February 16, 1968; *Orlando Sentinel*, February 17, 1968; *Jacksonville Florida Times Union*, February 17, 21, 1968; *Tallahassee Democrat*, February 17, 1968; *Pensacola Journal*, February 20, 27, 1968; *St. Petersburg*

Independent, February 24, 1968; *Miami Herald*, February 25, 1968; Cocoa *Today*, February 27, 1968; *Orlando Sentinel*, February 27, 1968; *Tampa Tribune*, February 23, 1968; Floyd T. Christian, Statement, February 26, 1968, Crisis News Release File, OCMS; *Summary of Events Prior to the 1968 Walkout*, ibid.; Christian, Statement, February 23, 1968, ibid.; *Pompano Beach Sun Sentinel*, February 22, 1968; *Miami Herald*, February 22, 1968; *Tampa Tribune*, February 23, 1968; Cocoa *Today*, February 23, 1968; Christian, *To Members of the State Cabinet*, February 20, 1968, Crisis News Release File, OCMS.

3. *St. Petersburg Times*, February 13, 1968; *Tallahassee Democrat*, February 18, 1968; *Orlando Sentinel*, February 18, 1968; *Tampa Tribune*, February 17, 18, 1968; *St. Petersburg Times*, February 18, 1968; *Miami Herald*, February 17, 1968. Most likely Kirk had found himself in agreement with the FEA on the inadequacy of the compromise package bill. *Tallahassee Democrat*, February 16, 1968; *Tampa Tribune*, February 17, 1968.

4. Constans to Cormier, January 31, 1973; *Jacksonville Florida Times-Union*, February 21, 1968; *Miami Herald*, February 21, 23, 1968; *New York Times*, February 21, 1968; *Miami News*, February 22, 1968; *Jacksonville Journal*, February 22, 1968; *Ft. Lauderdale Daily News*, February 25, 1968.

5. *St. Petersburg Times*, February 18, 1968; *Tallahassee Democrat*, February 18, 1968; *Jacksonville Journal*, February 22, 1968; *Tampa Tribune*, February 22, 1968; *Orlando Sentinel*, February 23, 1968; *Tallahassee Democrat* February 23, 1968; *Pensacola Journal*, February 24, 1968; *Pensacola Journal*, February 26, 1968; *Miami Herald*, February 26, 1968; Cocoa *Today*, February 17, 1968; *Orlando Sentinel*, February 27, 1968; Constans to Cormier, January 31, 1973. Just prior to this meeting Constans and other high-level FEA officials while admitting that they had under valued the bill by at least $32,000,000 asked for an independent audit of the amount in the bill. *Jacksonville Journals*, February 23, 1968; *Miami Herald*, February 24, 1968; *Orlando Sentinel*, February 23, 1968; *St. Petersburg Times*, February 23, 1968; *Tampa Tribune*, February 23, 1968. The two state senators at the meeting were Lawton Chiles and Senate Minority Leader Bill Young. These and other legislators were so effective in arguing for their version of the bill that Pat Tornillo, Dade CTA executive secretary, telegrammed Dade legislators telling them to "cease and desist" from visiting schools to

explain the compromise bill. *St. Petersburg Times*, February 24, 1968; *Miami Herald*, February 24, 1968.

6. Phil Constans to Arthur White, Bowling Green, Kentucky, June 12, 1973, in author's personal files. During the strike a South Florida newsman noted that Constans was acting like "Christian's office did not even exist." *Ft. Lauderdale Daily News*, February 25, 1968.

7. Constans to Cormier, January 31, 1973; Walkout Telegram File, (Phil Constans, Bowling Green, Kentucky).

8. Cocoa *Today*, February 27, 1968; *Ft. Lauderdale Daily News*, February 25, 1968; *Daytona Beach Morning Journal*, February 21, 1968; *Tampa Tribune*, 1968; *Clearwater Sun*, February 22, 1968. These efforts are recorded in hundreds of newspaper clippings filed in Crisis February-March File Drawer, OCMS.

9. Dauer, "Florida," pp. 98–99. The best summary of this position is: "The True Power Structure," *Jacksonville Florida Times-Union*, February 27, 1968.

10. Arthur O. White, interview with Francis Lunsford, May 3, 1973, DOE; *Tampa Tribune*, February 21, 25, 1968; *Orlando Sentinel*, February 26, 27, 1968. For the best summary of this style of news coverage see "Newsmen Run Out On Schools," *Miami Herald*, February 27, 1968. Accounts of public indignation for a typical strike day, February 22, were found in practically every paper surveyed: *Pinellas Park Post, Okaloosa News Journal, DeFuniak Springs Herald, Polk County Democrat, Eustis Lake Region News, Florida Keys Keynoter, St. Petersburg Independent, Orlando Sentinel, Jacksonville Florida Times Union, Panama City Herald* and *Tallahassee Democrat*.

11. *St Petersburg Times*, September 30, 1967; *Miaim Herald*, September 13, 16, 1967; White, Lunsford interview, May 3, 1973; *Jacksonville Journal*, February 27, 1968; *Jacksonville Florida Times-Union*, February 27, 1968; *Ft. Lauderdale Daily News*, February 26, 1968; *Tampa Tribune*, February 21, 23, 25, 1968.

12. *Orlando Sentinel*, February 17, 1968; *Tampa Tribune*, February 23, 1968; *Jacksonville Florida Times-Union*, February 26, 1968; *Ft. Lauderdale Daily News*, February 26, 1968; *Miami Herald* February 26, 27, 1968.

13. *Tampa Tribune* February 23, 1968; White, Lunsford interview, May 3, 1973; White, interview with Jack Stevens, June 5, 1973, DOE; Constans in a recent interview clarified that the Dade CTA remained loyal to the end. Arthur O. White,

telephone interview with Phil Constans, June 11, 1973, DOE.

14. *Ft. Lauderdale Daily News*, February 22, 1968; *Miami Herald*, February 24, 1968; Cocoa *Today* February 27, 1968; *Pensacola Journal*, February 27, 1968. Many other South Florida teachers were also arrested on these charges as well as for violations of antipicketing ordinances. *Miami Herald*, February 22, 1968.

15. White, Lunsford interview, May 3, 1973; Constans to Cormier, January 31, 1973.

16. *Time* (March 1, 1968), pp. 70–71; *Ft. Lauderdale Daily News*, February 21, 22, 1968; *Jacksonville Florida Times-Union*, February 21, 22, 1968; *Orlando Sentinel*, February 12, 1968; Cocoa *Today*, February 23, 1968; *Miami Herald*, February 22, 1968; *Tallahassee Democrat*, February 22, 1968; *Tampa Tribune*, February 24, 1968; *FEA News*, February 19, 1968. In one report given to State Treasurer Broward Williams, a member of the "Outlaw" motorcycle gang and a proprietor of a psychedelic shop substituted as teachers. J. J. Cramer, To All Cabinet Members, March 4, 1968, Crisis News Release File, OCMS.

17. *Jacksonville Florida Times-Union*, February 17, 1968; *Tampa Times*, February 17, 1968; *Tallahassee Democrat*, February 17, 22, 1968; *St. Petersburg Times*, February 17, 1968; *Ft. Lauderdale Daily News*, February 21, 1968; *Tampa Tribune*, February 10, 22, 23, 1968; Floyd T. Christian, Statements, February 20, 21, 23, 1968, Crisis News Release File, OCMS; Events Prior to the 1968 Teacher Walkout, ibid., 2; Christian, Statements February 26, 1968, ibid.; Christian, *To Members of the State Board of Education, February 27, 1968*, Memo, ibid., Christian, Statement, February 27, 1968, ibid.

18. *Orlando Sentinel*, February 17, 1968; White, Christian interview, May 21, 1973; *St. Petersburg Times*, February 18, 20, 1968; *Miami Herald*, February 17, 1968; *Daytona Beach Evening News*, February 19, 1968.

19. Christain, *To Members of the State Board of Education*, February 27, 1968; Dexter Hagman, Statement, February 29, 1968, Crisis FEA Statement, Correspondence File, OCMS; Christian, *Resolution to the State Board of Education*, March 1, 1968, Crisis Resolutions File, OCMS: *Tampa Times*, March 2, 1968; Christian, Address, *The Superintendents' Conference, Mars Hill, North Carolina, July 24, 1968*, Notebook 1967–1968, OPIS.

20. Floyd T. Christian, Emergency Memorandum, February 28,

1968, Crisis News Release File, OCMS; Governor's News Conference, February 29, 1968, (tape) Erxleben, DOE; *Jacksonville Journal*, March 1, 1968; *Jacksonville Florida Times-Union*, March 1, 1968; *Orlando Sentinel*, March 1, 1968; *Miami Herald*, March 1, 3, 1968; *West Palm Beach Post Times*, March 2, 1968; White, Friedman interview, May 18, 1973; Christian, News Conference, February 29, 1968, (tape) Erxleben, DOE; Duane Bradford of the *Lakeland Ledger* described the tone of Christian's voice which is substantiated by the Erxleben tape; *Lakeland Ledger*, March 1, 1968; Christian, Remarks at Press Conference, February 29, 1968, DOE.

21. Christian, Closing Comments at State Board of Education Meeting, March 1, 1968, Crisis News Release File, OCMS. White, Hopping interview, May 25, 1973. *Jacksonville Florida Times-Union*, March 3, 1968; *Tampa Tribune*, March 2, 1968; *Miami Herald*, March 2, 1968; J. M. Minton of the *Herald* claimed that State Treasurer Williams had maybe 20 telegrams, *Miami Herald*, March 2, 1968. However, Chuck Perry, education aide for Kirk, claimed that the governor had received 3,000 communications on the strike, most of them urging him to sign the bill, but since the disclosure of "secret negotiations," 90 percent urged the governor "not to give in." *Tampa Tribune*, March 3, 1968.

22. Duval County Board of Public Instruction, February 29, 1968, Erxleben Notebook; *Jacksonville Journal*, March 1, 1968; *Miami Herald*, March 2, 1968; *Sarasota Journal*, March 1, 1968; *Ft. Myers News Press*, March 1, 1968; *Lake Wales Daily Highlander*, March 1, 1968; *Pensacola Journal*, March 1, 1968; *Ocala Star Banner* March 1, 1968; *Ft. Lauderdale Daily News*, March 1, 1968; *Orlando Star*, March 1, 1968; *Winter Haven Daily News Chief*, March 1, 1968; *Clearwater Sun*, March 1, 1968; Florida School Board Association *Bulletin*, No. 23, March 15, 1968; *Tampa Tribune*, March 2, 1968. Two tapes of Superintendents' Meetings, Haydon Burns Auditorium, March 1, 1968, Erxleben; *Tallahassee Democrat*, March 2, 1968; Christian, Statement, March 1, 1968, Crisis News Release File OCMS. Another factor that might have influenced the defeat of Christian's compromise was a letter to Cabinet officials from the executive vice president of Associated Industries, the most powerful industrial group in Florida, asking them to see that all resignations submitted to county school boards be made effective immediately: "It is far better to endure pain briefly, than to allow

a cancerous growth to erode our basic system of government." Cass, "Politics and Education," p. 78.

23. *Orlando Sentinel,* February 22, 1968; *Tampa Tribune,* March 2, 1968; Constans to Cormier, January 31, 1973; White, Christian interview, May 21, 1973; Floyd Christian Press Conference, February 29, 1968, Crisis News Release File, OCMS.

24. White, Lunsford interview, May 3, 1973.

25. Floyd T. Christian, Recommendations, March 8, 1968, Crisis News Release File, OCMS; White, Stevens interview, June 5, 1973; Dexter Hagman, Statement, March 8, 1968, Crisis FEA File, OCMS.

26. Claude Kirk to Christian, Tallahassee, March 12, 1968; Christian to Kirk, Tallahassee, March 12, 1968, Crisis Governor Kirk File, OCMS.

27. Hundreds of newspaper accounts of local board actions against teachers are in file drawer Crisis Clippings February 26, March 24, 1968, OCMS. See especially *Jacksonville Florida Times-Union,* July 8, 1968. Indeed, FEA reports noted that even its president-elect Jane Arnold was "locked out" of her classroom by an aroused Pinellas County School Board. *The Florida Teacher,* 3 (April 1968): 1; *Phi Delta Kappan,* 49 (June 1968). The DOE kept daily accounts of the number of unemployed teachers until April 1, 1968. Crisis News Release File, OCMS.

28. Floyd Christian, Statement, March 11, 1968; Christian, Memorandum, March 11, 1968, Crisis News Release File, OCMS; White, Christian interview, May 21, 1973.

29. White, Lunsford interview, May 3, 1973; Constans to Cormier, January 31, 1973; *Orlando Sentinel,* February 21, 1968; *Tampa Tribune,* February 23, 1968.

30. White, Seay interview, May 19, 1973; White, Christain interview, May 21, 1973; Christian, Statement, March 20, 1968, Crisis News Release File, OCMS; Constans to Cormier, January 31, 1973; Christian to Dexter Hagman, March 13, 1968, Erxleben Notebook, DOE; Christian, Statement, April 1, 1968, ibid.; Christian, Recommendations, June 1, 1968, ibid.; *American Teachers,* September, 1968.

31. *Orlando Star,* February 12, 1969. The FEA membership loss due to the strike was estimated at fifteen thousand teachers, including all administrators, because the administrative section of the FEA had voted to become a separate independent organization; ibid. As for engaging in another strike, even stalwart FEA members warned that never again would they

go through such an ordeal. Moreover, Constans, after his dismissal in 1969, related that he opposed statewide strikes and preferred local actions; and the NEA for a time after the Florida setback seriously considered reinstating its no-strike provisions. Many predicted: "The Florida walkout last of its kind." *Education News*, April 22, 1968.

Chapter 5. Threshold of a New Era

1. Marshall Frinks, "Is Gut Judgement Enough?," *Florida Schools*, 30 (June 1968): 14–15; Floyd T. Christian, *Remarks to Group I Subcommittee–House Committee on Appropriations, March 24, 1971*; Legislature 1971 File, OC MS, p. 3.
2. Eldridge R. Collins, Howard J. Friedman, "The 1968 Special Session Legislature," *Florida Schools*, 30 (March 1968): 20.
3. Cliff Cormier, "When the Dust Settles: It Won't Be the Same," *Gainesville Daily Sun*, February 25, 1968.
4. *Tampa Tribune Times*, March 17, 1968; *Draft Proposed 1968 Constitution*, July 1968, Reorganization DOE File, OPIS, 5.
5. Speech Delivered by the Honorable Fred Schultz Speaker, House of Representatives Before the Organizational Session, November 12, 1968, xerox copy, Legislative Speeches 1968 File, OPIS.
6. Howard J. Friedman, "The New Legislature," *Florida Schools*, 33 (September–October 1970): 8; *Miami Herald*, April 4, 1971.
7. For an excellent diagram of Florida's reorganized government see "Meet Your Reshaped Florida Government," *St. Petersburg Times*, June 29, 1969; Eldridge R. Collins, Howard J. Friedman, "The 1969 Legislature," *Florida Schools*, 32 (September–October 1969): 23, 25.
8. Collins and Friedman, "1969 Legislature," 23–28; Christian, *Message to 1971 Legislature* p. 9; Arthur O. White, interview with Cecil Golden, November 14, 1973.
9. Floyd T. Christian, *State of Florida Department of Education and the Government Reorganization Act of 1969*, July 29, 1969, mimeograph, Reorganization DOE File, OPIS.
10. Bailey, *Index of Taxpaying Ability*; Floyd T. Christian, *Remarks to Joint Meeting of Senate Education Committee and House Public School Education Committee*, August 21, 1969, Pre-Legislature 1969 File, OPIS.
11. Christian, *Remarks to Joint Meeting of the House Public School Committee and the Senate Education Committee*,

August 21, 1968, p. 2; Arthur O. White, interview with Howard J. Friedman, October 24, 1973; *St. Petersburg Times*, February 13, 1971; Friedman, "1969 Special Session Helped Education," *Florida Schools*, 32 (January–February 1970): 25–26.

12. White, Christian interview, May 21, 1973; *Christian Biographical Data*, September 9, 1971.
13. Christian, *Remarks to Joint Meeting of the House Public School Committee and the Senate Education Committee*, August 21, 1968, *passim*.
14. *Transcript of a Joint Senate and House Education Committee Meeting*, Tampa, August 21, 1969, mimeograph, Pre-Legislature File, OPIS, pp. 13–35.
15. Howard J. Friedman, "One of the Most Important Sessions in Florida's History," *Florida Schools*, 33 (September–October 1970): 10–12; *St. Petersburg Times*, March 21, 1971.
16. Eldridge Collins, "Summary of Education Bills Passed in 1970 Legislature," *Florida Schools*, 33 (September–October 1970): 15; Christian, *Remarks to Sub-Committee . . . Appropriations*, March 24, 1971, pp. 9, 12.

Chapter 6. A New Era

1. Arthur O. White, Florida's Chief State School Officers and Federally Mandated School Desegregation 1954–1973, unpublished paper, August, 1973, DOE, pp.7, 12–13.
2. *Jacksonville Florida Times-Union*, March 30, 1971; *Miami News*, April 12, 1971; *Daytona Beach Morning Journal*, April 19, 1971; Floyd T. Christian, "There is a Shift in Emphasis," *Florida Schools*, 34 (September–October 1971): 13.
3. Erick Wentworth, "Plan Test of Competition by Schools," Smith and Kniker, *Myth and Reality*, pp. 330–332.
4. *St. Petersburg Times*, October 20, 1970; *Palm Beach Post Times*, December 6, 1970; *Tallahassee Democrat*, September 2, 1973.
5. *Tallahassee Democrat*, September 2, 1973; *Jacksonville Florida Times-Union*, January 11, 1971, September 22, 1967; Floyd T. Christian, Statement, July 27, 1971, Legislature 1971 File, OPIS.
6. *Jacksonville Florida Times-Union*, January 11, 1971. For the best summary of this position see Gregory Johnson, "Tax Reform Why Florida Needs It," *St. Petersburg Times*, March 21, 1971.

7. *Jacksonville Florida Times-Union*, January 23, 1971; *Jacksonville Journal*, February 9, 1971.
8. *Jacksonville Florida Times-Union*, January 22, 1971; *St. Petersburg Times*, February 13, 9, March 26, 1971; *Miami Herald*, April 4, May 23, 1971.
9. *St. Petersburg Times*, February 9, 1971.
10. *Gainesville Daily Sun*, January 24, 1971.
11. NEA, *Accountability*, mimeograph, author's file, Gainesville, Florida.
12. *Tallahassee Democrat*, February 11, 1971.
13. DOE, *Plan for Educational Assessment in Florida: Final Report* (Tallahassee, 1971), pp. 5—11.
14. Christian, *Remarks to Sub-Committee . . . Appropriations, March 24, 1971*, passim.
15. *St. Petersburg Times*, May 7, 1971; Cocoa *Today*, May 19, 1971; *Gainesville Daily Sun*, May 20, 1971; "Educational Accountability Act of 1971," *Florida Statutes*, Chapter 229 (Tallahassee, 1971): 57.
16. *St. Petersburg Times*, February 9, 13, March 26, June 6, April 2, May 9, 1971; *Jacksonville Florida Times-Union*, March 8, April 2, 1971; *Jacksonville Florida Times-Union and Journal*, March 14, 1971; Cocoa *Today*, March 21, 1971; *Gainesville Daily Sun*, May 4, 1971; *Miami Herald*, May 13, June 24, 1971; *Pensacola Journal*, June 17, 1971; Richard A. Pettigrew, *The Florida Legislature, 1971: Health and Vocational-Technical Education*, mimeograph, Legislature 1971 File, OPIS; Christian, "A Shift in Emphasis," p. 11.
17. *Gainesville Daily Sun*, August 31, 1971.
18. Christian, *Message to the 1971 Legislature*, 17; *Jacksonville Florida Times-Union*, August 12, 1971; *Improving Education in Florida: A Report by the Governor's Citizens' Committee on Education* (Tallahassee, 1971).
19. Reubin O'D. Askew, *Remarks to the Sarasota County Legislative Weekend, January 15, 1972* mimeograph, 1972 legislative clipping File, OPIS; 11—16; Askew, *Supplemental Message to the Florida Legislature, February 1, 1972*, mimeograph, ibid., pp. 3—5; *Miami News*, January 20, 1972, *Tallahassee Democrat*, January 19, 1972; *St. Petersburg Times*, January 30, 1972; *Orlando Sentinel*, February 3, 1972; *Pensacola News-Journal*, February 3, 1972; *St. Petersburg Times*, February 3, 5, 1972; *Tallahassee Democrat*, February 6, 7, 1972; *Miami Herald*, February 9, 1972; *Tampa Tribune*, February 4, 8, 9, 10, 1972. The first time the proposal came

up in the House it failed to achieve the 3/5ths margin by 2 votes; the second time it failed by 6 votes. *Tampa Tribune*, February 8, 1972.

20. *Daytona Beach Journal*, February 16, 1972; *St. Petersburg Times*, February 16, 18, 22, 24, March 3, 16, 1972; *Ft. Lauderdale Daily News*, February 16, 1972; *Jacksonville Times Union and Journal*, February 20, 1972; *Jacksonville Florida Times-Union*, February 24, 1972; *Palm Beach Post*, February 24, 1972; *The Pensacola Journal*, February 24, 1972; Cocoa *Today*, February 28, 1972; *Tampa Tribune*, March 22, 1972. The vote totals were: 1,127,631 in favor of a U. S. Constitutional amendment to prohibit forced busing for racial balance with 396,777 against and 1,095,872 in favor of equal educational opportunity for all with 293,775 against. Richard (Dick) Stone, *Tabulations of Official Votes Cast Presidential Preference Primary Election, March 14, 1972, and Special Election November 2, 1971*, Reubin Askew File, OCMS.

21. "A Florida Legislature 1973: Summary of Bills Dealing with Education," *Florida Schools*, 35 (September–October 1973): 12–13; W. Cecil Golden to Ben Brodinsky, Tallahassee, December 5, 1973, OPIS. In this letter, the Associate Commissioner for Planning and Coordination outlines his conception of the Florida strategy for comprehensive planning.

22. Floyd T. Christian, *Address FSBA-FADSS, Joint Meeting*, December 6, 1972, FTC Speeches 1973 File, OPIS.

23. Floyd T. Christian, "Commisioner of Education, A Message," *Florida Schools* 35 (September-October 1973): 10; Al Erxleben, "School Financing: It's All New," ibid., pp. 16–23.

24. Erxleben, "School Financing," pp. 18–19.

25. "Senate Bill No. 622," Chapter 73–338, *Laws of Florida* (Office of the Secretary of State, Florida): 18; "Summary of Bills . . . 1973"; Arthur O. White, interviews with Cecil Golden, December 12, 1972 and November 14, 1973.

26. Floyd T. Christian, *Address to Florida Association of Secondary School Principals*, October 8, 1973, FTC Speeches 1973 File, OPIS, pp. 3-4; Golden to Brodinsky, December 5, 1973.

27. "Summary of Bills . . . 1973," p. 15; White, Golden interview, November 14, 1973; Brodinsky to Golden, December 5, 1973, p. 2.

28. Floyd T. Christian, *Address to Chief State School Officers*, July 30, 1973, FTC Speeches 1973 File, OPIS.

Index